P9-CEK-896

"I Shall Return" —Jesus

Jerry Vines

This book is designed for your personal reading pleasure and profit. It is also designed for group study. A leader's guide with helps and hints for teachers is available from your local Christian bookstore or from the publisher at $1.95.

VICTOR BOOKS

a division of SP Publications, Inc., Wheaton, Illinois

Offices also in Fullerton, California • Whitby, Ontario, Canada • London, England

Bible quotations are from the King James Version unless otherwise noted. Other quotations are from *The New Scofield Reference Bible* © 1967 by the Delegates of the Oxford University Press, Inc., New York. Used by permission.

Library of Congress Catalog Card Number: 76-55631
ISBN: 0-88207-702-3

© 1977 by SP Publications, Inc. World rights reserved
Printed in the United States of America

VICTOR BOOKS
A division of SP Publications, Inc.
P. O. Box 1825 • Wheaton, Illinois 60187

Contents

1

Jesus' Second Coming

Early in World War II, U.S. PT Boat 41 and a B-17 bomber carried General Douglas MacArthur through Japanese-patrolled seas and skies from the Philippine Islands to the still-free land of Australia. There, in answer to reporters' questions, the leader of America's besieged forces in the Pacific war zone declared:

"The President of the United States ordered me to break through the Japanese lines and proceed from Corregidor to Australia for the purpose, as I understand it, of organizing the American offensive against Japan, a primary object of which is the relief of the Philippines. I came through and I shall return."

In October 1944 General MacArthur landed with his troops in the country he had left two years earlier and announced over a loudspeaker:

"People of the Philippines: I have returned. By the grace of Almighty God . . . we have come,

5

dedicated and committed to the task of destroying every vestige of enemy control over your daily lives. . . ."

The Philippines were soon liberated and the Japanese empire soon vanquished. The victorious commander had returned in power.

Today the whole world struggles against a spiritual oppressor. Men of good will seek peace, but wars increase. The good life of abundance beckons to mankind, but governmental corruption and energy shortages and racial conflict threaten real progress. Humanity yearns for love and understanding, but selfishness and pride dominate personal relationships. When shall we be freed and fulfilled?

The answer resounds in the reassuring words of Jesus: "I shall return." Jesus came to earth the first time as a Servant and as a Lamb—to suffer and to die as a Sacrifice for the corruption and sin of all men. Jesus is coming again as the Conqueror of all evil and the King of the universe He created! His triumphant return is as certain as His first coming, because God's revelation, the Bible, predicted both comings.

His Second Coming Was Foretold

The theme of Jesus' second coming is one of the greatest in the Bible. The importance of His return is established by the frequency and the intensity of the biblical references to this climactic event. Someone said that biblical revelation can be summarized in three simple statements about the Son of God: "He is coming; He has come; and He is coming again."

The return of Jesus Christ is foretold both in the Old Testament and the New. The patriarch Job affirmed: "I know that my Redeemer liveth, and that He shall stand at the latter day upon the earth" (Job 19:25). The psalmist declared, "When the Lord shall build up Zion, He shall appear in His glory" (Ps. 102:16).

Daniel's writing is full of still-future events, and he prophesied in the seventh chapter of his book that the Son of man, Jesus, would come to a glorious kingdom where all nations would serve Him. Daniel envisioned the establishment of this kingdom through warfare when the Messiah, like a great stone, would smash the nations of the world and rule the earth (2:34-35).

Zechariah described earth's last war in this way: "Then shall the Lord go forth and fight against those nations . . . and His feet shall stand in that day upon the Mount of Olives. . . . And the Lord shall be king over all the earth" (14:3-4, 9).

Jewish readers of the Old Testament clearly understood these prophecies of God's kingdom ruling the whole earth, but only a few perceived that the King would be God's eternal Son and that He would first come to earth as a man before He would return again as conquering King. This truth is seen in such passages as Isaiah 9. "For unto us a child is born, unto us a Son is given, and the government shall be upon His shoulder, and His name shall be called Wonderful, Counselor, the Mighty God, the Everlasting Father, the Prince of Peace. Of the increase of His government there shall be no end, upon the throne of David, and upon His kingdom, to order it, and to establish it with judgment and with justice from henceforth even forever" (6-7).

Jesus' first coming and the writings of His disciples in the New Testament unveiled this mystery: the God-Man must suffer and die so that a new chosen people, the Church, might live eternally with Him. Jesus' sacrificial death ended the Old Testament era of law, and inaugurated the New Testament age of grace: salvation through faith in Christ's atonement. New Testament writers refer to this cleared-up mystery:

"Of which salvation the prophets have inquired and searched diligently, who prophesied of the grace that should come unto you, searching what, or what manner of time the Spirit of Christ which was in them did signify, when it testified beforehand the sufferings of Christ, and the glory that should follow" (1 Peter 1:10-11). Jesus' suffering on the cross was the goal of His first advent; His glory as the monarch of the earth will be gained in His second advent.

New Testament writers make clear that it is Jesus who will come to earth as conquering Lord. Jesus Himself said: "The powers of heaven shall be shaken. And then shall they see the Son of man coming in a cloud with power and great glory" (Luke 21:26-27).

The writer of Hebrews affirms: "Christ was once offered to bear the sins of many; and unto them that look for Him shall He appear the second time without sin unto salvation" (Heb. 9:28).

The Apostle John, in his awesome revelations of the end times, reports: "I saw heaven opened, and behold a white horse; and He that sat upon him was called Faithful and True, and in righteousness He doth judge and make war . . . and His name is called The Word of God" (Rev. 19:11, 13b).

And in the next to the last verse of the Bible,

Jesus told John: "Surely I come quickly" (Rev. 22:20).

The coming of Jesus Christ is the hope of the ages—no one else can bring the righteousness and peace and joy that are promised in the kingdom of heaven (Rom. 14:17). You and I are witnessing a tottering civilization in the twentieth century. Leaders in finance, food production, and military affairs wonder when the mounting crises will collide and rip civilization apart. The worldwide collapse of freedom may not be far away, but the followers of Jesus Christ have a great hope in His return.

In Titus 2:13 this is called a "blessed hope"; in Hebrews 6:19, a hope which is "as an anchor of the soul, both sure and steadfast." Storms may swirl around the Christian, but he will not sink or crash on the rocks while he has the stabilizing hope of Jesus' return.

The coming of Jesus Christ is also a sanctifying hope. John wrote: "Every man that hath this hope in Him purifieth himself, even as He is pure" (1 John 3:3). The holy Son of God is coming back to escort His people to heaven, and those who are looking for Him want to be ready to welcome Him.

Preparation for the Event

When the late President Eisenhower was vacationing in Denver, Colorado, he heard of a six-year-old boy named Paul Haley who was dying of an incurable disease. The boy had expressed a desire to see the president and shake hands with him, and early on Sunday morning, the presidential limousine unexpectedly stopped in front of Paul's home. The president got out and went to the front door and knocked. It was opened by Mr. Haley, who stood dumbstruck at the sight of the president of the United States and the realization of his own sloppy appearance in T-shirt, worn shoes, and a day's growth of beard! Little Paul stood behind his father, and neither of them managed to say much as the famous army general and president talked for a few moments, shook hands, and departed. In the days that followed, Mr. Haley told friends about the exciting visit and his own shame in looking like a hobo before the president of the United States!

The Christian who is unprepared for Christ's return faces far greater remorse—not his clothes but his soul will be displayed to the Son of God. Will you be spiritually clean, eagerly receptive, and genuinely glad to see your Lord? Your expectancy of His return will help you to be ready.

In order to understand the Bible's prophecies about Jesus' second coming, we must learn to distinguish between some biblical similarities. Paul exhorted believers: "Study to show thyself approved unto God, a workman that needeth not to be ashamed, rightly dividing the word of truth" (2 Tim. 2:15). This verse means we learn to become faithful servants of God by properly understanding His Word, or "rightly dividing" God's teachings. By careful diligence and the illumination of the Holy Spirit, we see important distinctions in God's acts, directions, and plans. For instance, we should be careful to distinguish between Scriptures written primarily to the Jews, to Gentiles, and to the Church. In 1 Corinthians 10:32, we see this three-fold division of the human race. God acts and speaks in different ways toward these three groups, and you will understand the Bible better by always noting which group is the subject of a particular passage.

This does not mean we can ignore any part of the Word of God; the whole Bible is *for* us, but not all of the Bible is written *to* us. Sometimes the primary reference of Scripture is to the Jewish nation, and we may draw certain lessons from it for our lives while keeping in mind that it is written primarily to the Jews. Some passages are directed to the godless Gentiles, and we discern God's over-all plan for them without confusing the destiny of the Jews and the Church. And, of course, Scriptures addressed particularly to Christ's followers have different meaning for the other groups.

Another important distinction should be made between law and grace and kingdom. The law given on Mt. Sinai describes God's dealing with men before the first coming of Christ. The law and animal sacrifices were man's way to God. Now, as John said, "The law was given by Moses, but grace and truth came by Jesus Christ" (John 1:17). Men are saved by God's grace through faith in Christ. In the future kingdom age, all humanity will see and know the divine Ruler of the earth, but they will have to prove their love and loyalty in daily living.

A "Contradiction" Explained

To understand the deeper truths about Christ's second coming, it is essential that we are "rightly dividing the Word of truth" about His second coming. His return has two phases or two separate time-events. These two phases can be seen in the following two texts:

"But of the times and seasons, brethren, ye have no need that I write unto you. For yourselves know perfectly that the day of the Lord so cometh as a thief in the night. For when they shall say, Peace and safety, then sudden destruction cometh upon them, as travail upon a woman with child, and they shall not escape. But ye, brethren, are not in darkness, that that day should overtake you as a thief. Ye are all the children of light, and the children of the day; we are not of the night, nor of darkness. Therefore let us not sleep, as do others, but let us watch and be sober. For they that sleep, sleep in the night; and they that be drunken are drunken in the night" (1 Thes. 5:1-7).

And second, Revelation 1:7—"Behold, He cometh with clouds; and every eye shall see Him, and they also which pierced Him: and all kindreds of the earth shall wail because of Him."

The first passage refers to the coming of the Lord as being like a thief in the night. This implies that it is secretive and unnoticed. The second passage, by contrast, announces that every eye shall see Jesus returning, and the people of the earth shall wail at the sight. How can we distinguish these apparently contradictory descriptions of Christ's second coming? We reconcile them and understand the meaning when we realize there are *two phases* in Christ's return: two great events we will call the "Rapture" and the "Revelation."

Before we investigate these events closely, let me mention that there will be a seven-year period of time between the Rapture of the Church and the Revelation of the Lord. This seven-year period will be a time of great tribulation on earth—untold sorrow, unprecedented misery, and worldwide upheavals. We will look at this later in detail. During this time in heaven, two momentous things will take place: the Judgment Seat of Christ; and the Marriage Supper of the Lamb. Later on we will look more deeply into these also.

Now, let me contrast the two phases of Jesus' second coming. The Rapture is Jesus' coming *for* His saints; the Revelation is Jesus coming *with* His saints. The Rapture takes place in the air; the Revelation occurs on the earth. The Rapture is a catching away; the Revelation is an unveiling. The Rapture brings bliss to the people of God; the Revelation brings judgment to the nations and their citizens who have rejected God.

The two-phase interpretation of Christ's coming is called the pretribulation view. Some Christians expect Jesus to return in the middle of the seven-year tribulation period, and others believe Jesus will return only once, at the end of the Tribulation. We will be looking at many Scriptures that support the pretribulation view of Christ's return. One of these is Revelation 4:1.

The last word is Revelation 3 is "churches," and at that point the Church as a body of believers disappears from the text. Next we read: "After this I looked, and behold, a door was opened in heaven; and the first voice which I heard was as it were of a trumpet talking with me, which said, Come up hither, and I will show thee things which must be hereafter." In the margin of your Bible by this verse you may want to write the word "Rapture."

Much farther along, after reading of catastrophes on the earth and conflicts in the heavens, we see another "opening in heaven" described in Revelation 19:11-13. "And I saw heaven opened, and behold a white horse; and He that sat upon him was called Faithful and True, and in righteousness He doth judge and make war. His eyes were as a flame of fire, and on His head were many crowns; and He had a name written, that no man knew, but He Himself. And He was clothed with a vesture dipped in blood: and His name is called The Word of God."

This, of course, is Jesus! He is coming down out of heaven with his angelic armies to "smite the nations" and "rule them with a rod of iron" (Rev. 19:15). In the margin you may write the word "Revelation." Here are pictured the two phases of the coming of our Lord: the Rapture *for* His saints, catching them up to heaven; and His Revelation *with* His saints to rule the earth for a thousand years.

An illustration from history helps make this clear. The English people revolted against their government in the 1600s and asked Prince Charles, the son of an earlier king, to be the new ruler. Charles had been exiled to Europe, and he invited leading supporters to meet him in France. They crossed the channel and made plans for Charles II's rule in England. Then they returned together to establish the new monarchy. It came in two phases: the return for his supporters; and the return with his supporters. Now we want to look closely at the two key words, Rapture and Revelation.

The Rapture
The word Rapture itself does not appear in the Bible, but the concept is clearly there. In 1 Thessalonians we read: "The Lord Himself shall descend from heaven with a shout . . . then we which are

alive and remain shall be caught up . . . to meet the Lord in the air" (4:16-17).

"Caught up" is the English equivalent of *harpazo* in the Greek language of the New Testament. When this term was translated into Latin for Roman readers, the word used was *rapia,* and this is the root word for our English word, rapture. So, in an indirect way, the word "Rapture" is in the Bible.

This great Rapture of God's people could occur at any moment! Before you finish this day Jesus Christ could catch you away to heaven if you are a born-again child of God. I know of nothing in Scripture that requires our glorious hope of Christ's return to be delayed beyond today. We do not know the time of this Rapture, but we do know three things about it.

First, the Rapture will be sudden. In Mark 13 Jesus describes the events of the last days to His disciples, and He cautions: "But of that day and that hour knoweth no man, no, not the angels which are in heaven, neither the Son, but the Father" (v. 32). Anyone who sets a date for the coming of Christ is deceived. Such prophecies have proved to be false over and over again in history.

In 1843 William Miller and his congregation interpreted the Scriptures to say that the Lord was to return that year. The entire congregation sold their goods, clad themselves in white apparel and waited on a hilltop. When the Lord didn't appear they recalculated, decided they had made a one-year mistake, returned the next year only to be disappointed again. Others through the years have made the same kind of interpretations and have suffered the same kind of frustrations.

The doctrine of the Second Coming has come

into disrepute because of extreme interpretations and excessive dogmatism. Yet this is one of the most important doctrines in the Bible, so we must not neglect it. Jesus solemnly counseled His disciples:

"Take ye heed, watch and pray: for ye know not when the time is. For the Son of man is as a man taking a far journey, who left his house, and gave authority to his servants, and to every man his work, and commanded the porter to watch. Watch ye therefore: for ye know not when the master of the house cometh, at even, or at midnight, or at the cockcrowing, or in the morning: lest coming suddenly he find you sleeping" (Mark 13:33-36).

One of these days things will be proceeding as usual: banks will open in the morning for another business day; children will go to school for another slate of quizzes; mothers will face the daily tasks they've handled endlessly—but suddenly life will be different. Men and women and children who belong to Christ will instantly depart; individuals who lack a personal relationship to Christ will face a world governed by followers of Satan. Those who have debated a decision for Christ, but delayed, will find the escape route cut off. Jesus will have suddenly come and gone.

Second, Jesus' coming for His people will be secret. This was indicated in 1 Thessalonians 5 by comparison with "a thief in the night." I have never known a thief to call ahead and announce the time of his arrival. A thief plans to come when he is least expected; it's a guarded secret.

When the Rapture occurs for Jesus' saints, they are the only people who will see it. When the trumpet sounds and the Lord descends with a shout and the voice of the archangel, spiritually reborn people will be the only ones who hear. Naturally, families and governments will be stunned at the mysterious disappearance of individuals and groups from every part of the earth, but no one will understand who hasn't grasped the key in the Bible.

Third, Jesus' coming will be immensely significant—for both believers and unbelievers. This is confirmed in Matthew 24. "As the days of Noah were, so shall also the coming of the Son of man be. For as in the days that were before the Flood they were eating and drinking . . . and knew not until the flood came . . . so shall also the coming of the Son of man be. Then shall two be in the field; the one shall be taken, and the other left. Two women shall be grinding at the mill; the one shall be taken, and the other left" (vv. 37-41).

When the great flood occurred, only the people inside the ark with Noah escaped the devastation. When the Rapture occurs, only the born-again people of God will be taken away to safety.

Once a little girl rode an elevator with her mother, higher and higher in the Empire State Building. When they reached the eighty-sixth floor and still continued upward, the awed little girl murmured: "Does Jesus know we're coming?" Let me assure you that Jesus knows we are coming upward to meet Him in the Rapture.

When I was a boy, I used to visit a blacksmith's shop and watch the smithy make shoes for horses. Sometimes he would magnetize an iron shoe and let me play with it. I'd gather some metal shavings and steadily move the magnet toward them. The closer the magnet came, the more active the shavings became. When the gap was sufficiently closed, up the shavings leaped to the magnet! The magnetic attraction overcame gravity.

Today we are seeing many churches winning souls to Jesus Christ, many Bible studies attracting curious seekers, and many signs of renewal among Christians. I believe the reason is that Jesus' return is near. One of these days Jesus will be here—and gone. If you are saved from your sins, you will be included in the group that is taken. If you are still lost in your sins, you will stay behind in the group that is tragically left.

Imagine living in a world where there is the memory of goodness but little power to perform it. What disorders and fears will lurk in a world where people no longer pray to a God of justice and generosity? People who think they have already experienced their personal "hell" on earth will suddenly find they have lots of company—but no comfort.

After the Rapture, the "man of sin" (2 Thes. 2:3), or Antichrist, will offer himself as the world's savior. He will promise peace to war-panicked peoples, order for lawless cities, and food for starving populations. Desperately they will accept him as supreme leader—only to discover his ghastly deception when it is too late.

According to Scripture, the world will have a mock peace for three and one-half years. Then the Antichrist will reveal his true character and demand total submission and even worship. The worldwide idolatry will trigger God's wrath, and the calamities that envelop the earth will cause men to gnash their teeth in pain—but they will not repent of their evil. Satan-inspired hatred of God will make these rebels eternally hopeless and helpless.

The Revelation

A number of Scriptures help us understand the second phase of Jesus' coming. "Behold, the Lord cometh with ten thousands of His saints" (Jude 14). And, "He cometh with clouds" (Rev. 1:7). Turbulence is depicted in the distant skies. "Immediately after the tribulation of those days shall the sun be darkened, and the moon shall not give her light, and the stars shall fall from heaven, and the powers of the heavens shall be shaken. And then shall appear the sign of the Son of man in heaven, and then shall all the tribes of the earth mourn, and they shall see the Son of man coming in the clouds of heaven with power and great glory" (Matt. 24:29-30).

Second Thessalonians presents the Revelation of Christ while 1 Thessalonians deals primarily with the Rapture. In 2 Thessalonians 1:7 we read: "To you who are troubled, rest with us, when the Lord Jesus shall be revealed from heaven with His mighty angels." God's people, the saints, will accompany Christ back to earth, but God's powerful angels will fight against the armies of earth. These majestic ambassadors from heaven always attend the great events of God.

When Jesus was born, angels sang His praise to earthlings. In the garden of temptation, an angel came and strengthened Christ after His physical and spiritual ordeal. When the crucified Jesus lay in a sealed tomb, an angel came and rolled away the stone from the door. And one of these days, the Saviour will appear again, not in humiliation, but in irresistible power with legions of relentless angels.

Their mission is pitiless: "In flaming fire taking vengeance on them that know not God, and that obey not the Gospel of our Lord Jesus Christ; who shall be punished with everlasting destruction from the presence of the Lord" (2 Thes. 1:8-9). The Saviour who came to die for His enemies returns as Judge of the unrepentant. Men who will not voluntarily live for God will exist forever apart from Him.

Then the Christian finds an amazing encouragement in verse 10: "He shall come to be glorified in His saints." Notice that the glory spoken of here belongs to the *followers* of Jesus! This is amplified in Colossians 3:4—"When Christ, who is our life, shall appear, then shall ye also appear with Him in glory." Christians don't rank very high on this world's scales; they are considered fanatics or fools or weaklings, but their day is coming! When Jesus returns He is going to exhibit His saints as the reason for His joy and the proof of His love. Further, "If we suffer, we shall also reign with Him" (2 Tim. 2:12). That's the tremendous prospect for believers!

What is your response toward the coming Rapture and Revelation? If you are a Christian who wants the most out of your future, you should focus your heart on Christ's return and live every day in the light of His coming glory.

Paul informs us: "There is laid up for me a crown of righteousness, which the Lord, the righteous Judge, shall give me at that day; and not to me only, but unto all them also that love His appearing" (2 Tim 4:8). England's Queen Victoria said, "Oh, I wish that the Lord Jesus would return in my lifetime; I would so much like to lay my crown at His feet." You will have a heavenly crown to honor Him if you devoutly yearn for His return.

A true desire to see Jesus brings changes in our lives. Paul described them this way in Titus 2:12-13 —"Denying ungodliness and worldly lusts, we should live soberly, righteously, and godly, in this present world; looking for that blessed hope and the glorious appearing of the great God and our Saviour Jesus Christ." There are both positives and negatives in this holy preparation.

And what is your response if you have never trusted this returning Saviour? Only you can answer, but I urge you to heed the Bible's warning: "Now is the day of salvation." "Why will you die . . .? Turn yourselves and live" (2 Cor. 6:2; Ezek. 18:31-32).

Many years ago Orson Wells produced a radio drama of an imaginary attack from outer space. A student at Campbell College in North Carolina turned on his radio midway through the broadcast and did not realize he was hearing a fictitious report. When the announcer vividly described fire falling upon the earth, the student recalled some sermons from his boyhood years and concluded that the end of the world had come. He grabbed the telephone and called home, saying: "Mama, Mama, have you got your radio on? The fire is falling, the end of the world is coming, and I'm not ready to meet God!" The next morning he was the object of jokes and teasing around the campus.

But in the chapel service a godly Bible teacher took the podium and said, "I understand that one of the boys got a lot of ribbing because he got scared listening to the radio program last night. But, young men and women, what if it had truly been the end of the world last night—would you be ready?"

Seven unprepared young people got ready that morning by receiving Jesus Christ into their hearts. If He comes back today, are you ready? Can you joyfully and confidently respond with John the apostle: "Even so, come, Lord Jesus"?

2

Times Are
A-Changing

How far could you travel in today's world if you
couldn't read signs? There's an array of signs on
the highways, a forest of signs in airport terminals,
and a chaos of signs in any town business district.
Anyone who reads the signs can find his way, and
following the same route over and over acquaints
the traveler with details that take shape as a pattern. Sighting a landmark assures the traveler that
another recognized object is just ahead.

Jesus traced the sign-pattern of final world events
for His disciples as He talked to them on the slope
of the Mount of Olives. This famous mountain
rises on the east side of Jerusalem, just across the
Kidron Valley. After Jesus' resurrection from the
grave, He ascended to heaven from the top of
Mount Olivet. The prophet Zechariah predicted
that the Lord would descend on this same Mount
of Olives to battle the assembled armies of the
world (Zech. 14:3-4). But the mountainside was

peaceful on the day that Jesus gave His "Olivet discourse," a frightening description of the world's last days.

The discourse began when Jesus pointed to the beautiful temple and informed the disciples that it faced certain destruction. Perhaps the disciples were somewhat breathless as they asked: "When shall these things be? And what shall be the sign of Thy coming, and of the end of the world?" (Matt. 24:3). Then Jesus began to paint the picture of the future.

"Take heed that no man deceive you. For many shall come in My name, saying, I am Christ; and shall deceive many. And ye shall hear of wars and rumors of wars; see that ye be not troubled; for all these things must come to pass, but the end is not yet. For nation shall rise against nation, and kingdom against kingdom: and there shall be famines, and pestilences, and earthquakes, in divers places. All these are the beginning of sorrows. . . . Now learn a parable of the fig tree: When his branch is yet tender, and putteth forth leaves, ye know that summer is nigh; so likewise ye, when ye shall see all these things, know that it is near, even at the doors" (Matt. 24:4-8; 32-33).

It is interesting to note that significant new movements of God on earth and His divine interventions are accompanied by wonders and miraculous signs. When God created this world, indescribable power was demonstrated on the earth and in the heavens. When God gave the law to Moses, fire and smoke and earthshaking forces signaled the beginning of a new dispensation. In the days of Elijah and Elisha, God performed miracles and wonders that confirmed His divine message through the prophets. When Jesus Christ came into this world and opened the age of grace, signs in the skies and miracles on the earth announced God's interruption of ordinary events. And the Bible assures us that supernatural marvels will accompany Jesus' return to earth. Before He returns, Jesus said, worldwide developments will foreshadow His second coming. These unprecedented conditions will serve as signs pointing to Jesus' return.

Although no human knows the exact time of Christ's return, the signs of the end times tell us when the great event is approaching. There are no signs, of course, pointing to the rapture of God's people from the earth—we are to be constantly listening for the Lord's shout that will call us to heaven. But since the revelation of Christ to earth follows the Rapture by only seven years, the signs marking the end of history can stir our hearts in anticipation for our returning Lord. The following paragraphs discuss some of the signs.

Multiplication

The first sign takes us back to Genesis 1:27-28. "So God created man in His own image, in the image of God created He him; male and female created He them. And God blessed them, and God said unto them, Be fruitful and multiply, and replenish the earth, and subdue it." The word "replenish" could be translated "fill the earth." One of God's purposes was for man to fill the earth, and the current population explosion is an indication to us of the coming again of our Saviour.

Today the experts are warning us about the need to protect our environment and conserve our resources. Specialists predict that unless population growth is halted, the human race is doomed.

One of the suggested solutions is a legal restriction on the number of children in families. Parents of more than two children would be prosecuted and sterilized. This radical proposal is one of many heard these days for coping with a world population crisis.

It is true that our world is rapidly filling up with people. During the Stone Age, there were perhaps ten million people on earth. In the time of Jesus, world population was approximately three million. Today there are over four *billion* people on earth, and if the present rate of increase continues, there may be over six billion people by the year 2000.

When people are proliferating and streaming into cities, inevitable problems arise. Overcrowding, crime, unemployment, and overflowing courts and jails all strain the capacity of municipal systems to maintain an orderly society.

Our Saviour predicted that before His return there would be famines and pestilences and earthquakes in many places. It is estimated that half of the people in the world go to sleep hungry every night. Countless thousands are dying of starvation or malnutrition every day. There are simply too many people to feed in many areas of the world today.

In Jesus' prediction, He went on to say: "As the days of Noah were, so shall also the coming of the Son of man be." Genesis 6:1 reveals that the multiplying of people was a characteristic of Noah's time. Wickedness increased with the population expansion until God intervened to halt the corruption by the Flood. A similar scene is forming before our eyes. The multiplication sign is looming larger and larger on the world horizon.

Moon

Our Saviour, in talking about the end time signs, said: "And there shall be signs in the sun, and in the moon, and in the stars; and upon the earth distress of nations, with perplexity; the sea and the waves roaring" (Luke 21:25).

We know from the opening chapter of the Word of God (Gen. 1:14), that the moon was intended for a sign as well as for a timepiece of the seasons and days and years.

The prophet Joel tells us that "The sun shall be turned into darkness, and the moon into blood, before the great and the terrible day of the Lord come" (2:31). Modern scientists find that hard to believe, but in recent years Soviet physicists have discovered a gradual reddening of the moon surface. We don't know how God will turn the sun black and the moon red, but I think man's landing on the moon and exploration of outer space give us an indication of the end of the age. It is explained by a prophecy of Daniel.

Near the end of Daniel's amazing visions, an angel told him: "But thou, O Daniel, shut up the words, and seal the book, even to the time of the end; many shall run to and fro, and knowledge shall be increased" (Dan. 12:4). Some Bible commentaries have translated this last phrase as: "A knowledge explosion shall occur at the end of the age."

Did you know that human knowledge is doubling every ten years? Every 15 years the amount of printed material doubles. The remarkable scientific achievements all around us exhibit a fantastic growth of knowledge.

Consider the laser beam. It was invented about 15 years ago and is serving medicine and industry and communications in amazing ways. By concentrating light rays in a narrow beam, the laser generates terrific heat to cut steel or fuse a detached retina in the eye.

Electronic computers have greatly accelerated the growth of knowledge in the past thirty years. They store vast quantities of information for instant recall, perform complex mathematical calculations, and control the intricate operations of machinery. Without computers, space flight would be impossible.

Knowledge has always been dangerous when used for the wrong purpose. Satan is the most terrible example. As a mighty angel, God's supreme creation, he vowed rebelliously: "I will ascend into heaven, I will exalt my throne above the stars of God" (Isa. 14:13). God's response was: "Thou shalt be brought down to hell" (14:15).

Humanity's first civilization after the Great Flood defied God's command to resettle the earth and instead built a tower to demonstrate their skill, knowledge, and independence from God (Gen. 11:4-6). God's answer was a miraculous confusion of their language, dividing their knowledge and scattering them across the world. In the same way the moon and space travel may be a sign of the soon return of our Lord to answer our seeming independence.

Moral
A third sign can be seen all around us: the sign

of morality. Look at Jesus' words, "Iniquity shall abound, the love of many shall wax cold" (Matt. 24:12).

We all know that iniquity or sin is not an invention of the twentieth century, but the Bible predicts there will be intensified lawlessness and rebellion at the end of the age.

Consider the moral scene in America today. Crime is increasing at a rate called "epidemic" by the Federal Bureau of Investigation. The court dockets and prisons are so full that many law-breakers are set free to await their trial—and commit further crimes against an inadequately protected public. Famous lawyers openly declare their goal is obtaining the best deal possible for their client, not justice. Organized mobsters use violence and murder to control multimillion-dollar illegal businesses—and occasionally go to jail for income tax fraud.

Another deadly enemy is alcohol. Fifty percent of the fatal auto accidents in America involve drinking drivers. There are over nine million alcohol addicts in America—they would like to stop drinking but they can't. Alcohol is the most abused drug in America, not marijuana or heroin; and alcohol is the number one choice of youthful drug users. Drunkenness is becoming a serious problem in many high schools.

Our generation is described as "the permissive society." We prefer to let people do what they want to rather than conform to "old-fashioned" standards. The circulation of *Playboy* and other sex-saturated magazines is higher than the leading news magazines. Films boast of their X-rated morality, and rock music stars tantalize millions of young fans with songs like "Let's Spend the Night Together." The entertainment world knows nothing that is sacred—life is a carnival and people are simply animals. Jesus said iniquity will abound, and the sign of morality indicates that the coming of Jesus Christ is near.

Merger

No matter how depraved humanity becomes, it always has its religion and false gods. The Bible informs us that a sign of the last days will be efforts to unite the religions of the world. I call this the merger sign.

The Apostle Paul gives a clue about the timing of the Day of the Lord, "Let no man deceive you by any means; for that day shall not come, except there come a falling away first" (2 Thes. 2:3). "Falling away" comes from the Greek word *apostasia*, from which we get the word "apostasy" in English. It means to turn away from the sacred faith.

For further insight consider this statement: "Now the Spirit speaketh expressly, that in the latter times some shall depart from the faith, giving heed to seducing spirits, and doctrines of devils" (1 Tim. 4:1). Here again we see apostasy predicted as apparent believers "depart from the faith" to follow the doctrines of evil spirits.

We have all seen some of this: ministers and theology scholars denying the virgin birth of Jesus, His bodily resurrection, and even the existence of God. These leaders profess to be Christians, but they promote the teaching of demons. Jude wrote about such men who would creep into the church unnoticed and end up "denying the only Lord God and our Lord Jesus Christ" (v. 4). In American Protestant churches the word for merger is ecumenical. This comes from the Greek word *oikoumene,* which means the inhabited earth. The hope of many Protestant leaders is the union of all Christian churches. After that, their doctrines could easily stretch to include all the religions of the world. In Revelation 13 we have the Apostle John's vision of two unusual beasts. Without going into detail, you will notice that the first beast had seven heads and ten horns (v. 1). The following verses show that this beast represents a world government. Then, verse 11 says: "And I beheld another beast coming up out of the earth; and he had two horns like a lamb, and he spake as a dragon." The combined characteristics of a lamb and a dragon remind us of a wolf in a sheepskin: it pictures a representative of a ravenous world religion. The word "worship" in the chapter, depicts the enforced reverence for this enemy of God. Religion will then be exposed as Satan's greatest deception.

If you belong to a church group that favors union with other groups more than faithfulness to biblical doctrines, I advise you to leave that church. There is no such thing as union of all of the faiths in this world. The Bible challenges, "How can two walk together except they be agreed?" You can tie two cats' tails together and get union but you won't have unity.

If you are born again by the Spirit of God and your sins are washed away in the blood of Jesus Christ, you are truly united with the fellow believers who will meet in the sky when the trumpet is sounded for us. Just be sure you're a member of the true Church, Jesus' spiritual body.

Market

Surely you've heard of the European Common Market, the nine-nation federation that coordinates economic policies for the benefit of all its members. I believe this is the forerunner of history's last empire. To see why, let's turn back to the Book of Daniel.

Nebuchadnezzar, the king of Babylon, was given a dream by God of a huge statue of four different kinds of materials. "This image's head was of fine gold, his breast and his arms of silver, his belly and his thighs of brass, his legs of iron, his feet part of iron and part of clay" (2:32-33). The king couldn't understand the dream, or even remember its details, but God revealed the dream and its meaning to Daniel, the king's prisoner of war from Israel.

The head represented the Babylonian empire of Nebuchadnezzar; the silver chest and arms the kingdom that would conquer Babylon (which turned out to be Medo-Persia); the brass torso a third kingdom (Greece); the iron legs and feet another world kingdom (Rome). Daniel went on to explain that the fourth kingdom would be divided, "And in the days of these kings shall the God of heaven set up a kingdom, which shall never be destroyed; and the kingdom shall . . . consume all these kingdoms" (2:44).

We read in Revelation 13:1 of a world federation of nations that had ten horns and in Daniel we see that the last kingdom before God's kingdom has ten "toes." That kingdom was Rome, and so it is reasonable to conclude that the old Roman empire will be rebuilt in the last days. I am not saying the European Common Market is the group of federated nations predicted by Daniel and the Apostle

John, but it is worthy of your consideration. When Great Britain, Ireland, and Denmark joined the Common Market in 1973, the federated nations rose to nine. The other members are Italy, France, Belgium, The Netherlands, Luxembourg, and West Germany. Statesmen in all these countries envision a future political coalition that will be a United States of Europe. Eventually, a kingdom covering this area will produce the world dictator called Antichrist in the Bible. He will wield life-and-death control over every citizen. "He causeth all, both small and great, rich and poor, free and bond, to receive a mark in their right hand or in their foreheads; that no man might buy or sell, save he that had the mark, or the name of the beast, or the number of his name" (Rev. 13:16-17). Have you ever noticed how much we are living by numbers? I'm a social security number, I'm a credit card number, and I'm a bank account number. One of these days there is going to be a number written on the bodies of people who want to stay alive in the Antichrist's kingdom. If you are not ready for the rapture of the Church, you'd better be ready for the registration of Antichrist which will turn you into a number. You'll be one number among millions, but at least you'll get food to stay alive—so you can serve the Antichrist in his doomed army. The market sign is indeed an ominous one.

Military

Another sign anyone can read is plainly announced by Jesus: "Ye shall hear of wars and rumors of wars" (Matt. 24:6). War, of course, is not new. In the last 34 centuries of recorded history there have been only 268 years without war somewhere on earth. But warfare will be a way of life in the last days. Jesus added: "Nation shall rise against nation, and kingdom against kingdom . . . all these are the beginning of sorrows" (24:7-8).

Atomic weapons have radically changed warfare since the first military use of the atom bomb ended World War II in 1945. Recalling the nuclear devastation in Japan, General Douglas MacArthur warned the world: "If we do not now devise some greater and more equitable system, Armageddon will be at our door."

MacArthur was not trying to interpret Bible prophecy, but he saw clearly the horrible future facing warring nations. The Bible says Armageddon is real, and it will be the war of all wars exploding on the great plain of Megiddo in northern Israel. You can't miss the military sign.

Miracle

The last sign that makes me believe the coming of Jesus is near is the miracle sign, which I apply to the nation of Israel. New nations are rather commonplace these days. The continent of Africa is full of newly liberated countries. But when have you heard of a people expelled from their land for 2,000 years then returning and reestablishing their sovereignty in the same territory? It has never happened—except with the Jewish people in 1948.

Such an accomplishment was so incredible that only a few Bible students took literally the Old Testament prophecies about the dispersed Jews returning to their ancient homeland and forming a modern nation in Israel. I found a book by Increase Mather, the great Puritan preacher in the American Colonies, who said in 1669 that the Jews would be restored to Israel before the return of Jesus Christ. He and some other Bible teachers simply believed the Scripture prophecies despite the contrary evidence surrounding them.

Look at Jesus' words that signaled this astounding event almost 2,000 years ago. Speaking of the Jewish people, He said, "And they shall fall by the edge of the sword, and shall be led away captive into all nations: and Jerusalem shall be trodden down of the Gentiles, until the times of the Gentiles be fulfilled" (Luke 21:24). In A.D. 70 the Roman army destroyed Jerusalem after a long siege and exiled countless survivors to foreign lands. The Jewish nation was obliterated.

Persecuted, expelled, and massacred for 1,900 years in their adopted countries, a few Jewish leaders under Theodor Herzl organized the Zionist Movement at the beginning of this century. Their efforts culminated in the restoration of their nation in May 1948. Since then, large Arab armies tried to destroy Israel, but sank like Goliath against David. At the end of the Six Day War the temple area of Jerusalem had been captured by Israeli troops, and the Jewish capital was freed from Gentile control. We are living in the age Jesus predicted. He could return any day, though we set no dates for His coming. But we keep in our hearts His words: "When these things begin to come to pass, then look up, and lift up your heads; for your redemption draweth nigh" (Luke 21:28).

3

Reentry

When the space astronauts have completed a mission and are preparing to reenter the earth's atmosphere, earthlings anxiously await the successful return. Within a few suspenseful minutes the world knows whether pioneering humans have again conquered outer space. Interplanetary travel is a marvelous accomplishment, but this "giant step for mankind" is a flea's hop compared to the celestial trip we believers are going to take with Jesus!

Of course, many people scoff at the possibility of such an event. That shouldn't surprise us. The Apostle Peter predicted: "There shall come in the last days scoffers, walking after their own lusts, and saying, Where is the promise of His coming? For since the fathers fell asleep, all things continue as they were from the beginning of the creation" (2 Peter 3:3-4). These skeptics don't realize that God visited earth 1,900 years ago in the person of Christ, and that He will literally return again.

Anyone who is willing to investigate the Scriptures can discover this tremendous truth. The Old Testament prophets predicted that a descendant of David would become King of the earth, that He would be born of a virgin in Bethlehem, and that He would fulfill many signs. Jesus fulfilled all these prophecies, and the further prophecies about His second coming will come true just as precisely and completely.

In the New Testament we find Jesus' return related to His going to heaven after His resurrection. "As He went up, behold, two men stood by them in white apparel; which also said, 'Ye men of Galilee, why stand ye gazing up into heaven? This same Jesus, which is taken up from you into heaven, shall so come in like manner as ye have seen Him go into heaven'" (Acts 1:10-11).

Jesus' Ascension was a literal event, and His return will also be literal. Jesus Christ ascended bodily; He will return bodily. His departure was visible; His return will be visible—though the first phase for His people will not be seen by unbelievers.

As I understand the prophetic Scriptures, the next event on God's calendar is the return of Jesus in the air and His catching up of all born-again individuals. Regardless of denominational affiliation, every person who knows Jesus as Saviour is a member of His spiritual body; each one will hear His sudden call to meet Him in the air. I want to point out three thrilling truths about this next great event.

Rapture Depicted

The Rapture, as we've said earlier, is portrayed

in the Bible even though the word is not used. Let's read again. First Thessalonians 4:16-17—"The Lord Himself shall descend from heaven with a shout . . . and the dead in Christ shall rise first; then we which are alive and remain shall be caught up together with them in the clouds, to meet the Lord in the air." The Greek word *harpazo*, means to seize hastily, to snatch oneself, or to rescue from impending danger. It carries with it the idea of ecstasy, joy, or delight. The word is also used in other passages in the Word of God: "And to wait for His Son from heaven, whom He raised from the dead, even Jesus, which delivered (raptured) us from the wrath to come" (1 Thes. 1:10). In 2 Corinthians the Apostle Paul talks about an experience he had when he was caught up into the third heaven. He uses the same word. He was caught up, raptured; he was in an ecstasy and saw things which were not lawful for a man to utter (12:2-4). When we use the word "rapture" we are talking about that catching up of the people of God. We are talking about the literal and the actual transformation of every living believer when Jesus comes. Their miraculous flight becomes "rapture," signifying both a carrying away and a blissful experience.

Several illustrations of the Rapture are given in the Word of God. In Genesis 5 we are told that the sixth generation after Adam is represented by Enoch. His ancestors lived a certain number of years, then died. But Enoch was different, for he "walked with God, and he was not; for God took him" (5:24). This is explained in Hebrews 11:5— "By faith Enoch was translated that he should not see death; and was not found, because God had translated him: for before his translation he had this testimony, that he pleased God." What God did for Enoch shortly before the great flood He is going to do for a whole generation of believers when Jesus Christ raptures His Church.

There is a second illustration in the Old Testament, Elijah. The Bible tells us that Elijah was carried up to heaven in a chariot of fire in a whirlwind. You recall that Elijah fled into the desert to escape the wicked Queen Jezebel. There he prayed, "Take away my life; for I am not better than my fathers" (1 Kings 19:4). So far as I am able to find, this is the only prayer of Elijah's that was not answered. God postponed his departure date and then sent a fiery celestial vehicle! We ought never dictate to God when we are to leave this world; His timing will be perfect for you—perhaps at the return of Christ to earth; then you also will escape death!

Perhaps you have not realized how closely you are identified with Christ as a believer in Him. Through faith, believers are joined spiritually to Christ; Paul makes the amazing statements that we died with Him when He died on the cross, we were buried with Him when He went into the tomb, and we were raised with Him to walk in newness of life! (Rom. 6:3-4) Some day our bodies will duplicate the ascension of our Lord, and we will be reunited bodily with Him in the heavens!

Man is now able to travel about 25,000 miles per hour in space. With the thrust of powerful rocket engines we have managed to step to the nearest planet. Is it so incredible that the Creator of the men who made rocket engines can transport all of His people to heaven? The rapture depicted in the past indicates how it's going to be in our future!

Rapture Detailed

Our text, 1 Thessalonians 4:13-18, gives us a detailed description of the Rapture. The believers in Thessalonica had become Christians through Paul's preaching and had grown rapidly in their faith. Paul taught them many truths, then moved on to other cities. Within two years, scholars tell us, Paul put many of his teachings into permanent form in his first letter to the Thessalonian church.

Part of Paul's letter answers questions these young believers had in their minds. What happens to loved ones who have died before Jesus comes again? Their anxiety reveals that these early believers were already expecting Jesus' return! Would the dead ones miss out on the Rapture?

Not wanting the Christians to sorrow for the dead like people who had no hope of eternal life, Paul began to explain. "If [since] we believe that Jesus died and rose again, even so them also which sleep in Jesus will God bring with Him" (v. 14). The resurrection of Jesus is the guarantee of *our* resurrection! Paul goes on to say that the bodies of deceased believers will be caught up from their graves at the same time living believers are translated to the heavens. Elsewhere in Scripture we are told that the spirits of these deceased believers have already joined the Lord in heaven (2 Cor. 5:6-8; Phil. 1:21-23).

Then Paul describes our Lord's return. "The Lord Himself shall descend. . . ." In the original language the pronoun "Himself" is at the beginning of the sentence in the emphatic position. There will be no messenger: Jesus Christ *Himself* is coming! This is why death for the believer cannot be considered as the second coming of Christ. Also, the day of Pentecost cannot be the second coming of Jesus. Jesus Himself will welcome us into heaven and His glory.

There are three sounds associated with the coming again of our Lord. We are told there will be a shout, a voice of the archangel, and the trumpet of God. The "shout" evidently comes from Jesus, "Marvel not at this: for the hour is coming, in which all that are in the graves shall hear His voice" (John 5:28).

Later Jesus stood before the tomb of Lazarus, who had been dead four days, and called, "Lazarus, come forth." I agree with the country preacher who said, "If Jesus had not called Lazarus by his first name, every dead believer in that graveyard would have come forth!" Lazarus heard him and came out!

And there is the voice of the archangel. In the Book of Jude we are told about Michael the archangel guarding the body of Moses from Satan. It may be that when the Lord shouts from heaven the power of an attending angel will resurrect buried and disintegrated bodies.

In the Old Testament, trumpets were often used by the people of Israel to signal "Advance," "Retreat," or "Assemble." When Jesus descends from heaven, He will shout, the archangel will speak, and the trumpet of God will sound!

When I first started preaching, I thought Jesus would come from heaven and raise everybody at the same time, then all would stand before the throne of God for judgment. If you were saved, you'd go into heaven; and if you were lost, you'd go into hell. But as I studied the Bible further I saw that there are *two* resurrections taught in the Word of God.

The reality of resurrection is clearly taught in the Old Testament. "And many of them that sleep in the dust of the earth shall awake, some to everlasting life, and some to shame and everlasting contempt" (Dan. 12:2). At this point of disclosure about the future life, the resurrection for everyone seems to be one event.

In the New Testament Jesus began to reveal further details. He said, ". . . All that are in the graves shall hear . . . and shall come forth; they that have done good, unto the resurrection of life; and they that have done evil, unto the resurrection of damnation" (John 5:28-29). But moments before that He had said: "The dead shall hear the voice of the Son of God, and they that hear shall live" (v. 25). Some will hear Christ's voice, and some will not!

After Jesus' Resurrection and Ascension, the Apostle Paul wrote about the resurrection of God's people. His description in 1 Corinthians 15 is the greatest presentation in the Bible on this subject. This chapter teaches we will have new resurrection bodies, bodies like Jesus' glorified body. Paul wrote: "As in Adam all die, even so in Christ shall all be made alive. But every man in his own order: Christ the firstfruits; afterward they that are Christ's at His coming" (vv. 22-23). This is the first resurrection—the resurrection of believers— which will be completed when new believers during the tribulation are killed, and Jesus brings them to heaven. They are described in Revelation 20:4-5 with a hint of the second resurrection.

"And I saw thrones, and they sat upon them, and judgment was given unto them: and I saw the souls of them that were beheaded for the witness of Jesus, and for the Word of God, and which had not worshiped the beast, neither his image, neither had received his mark upon their foreheads, or in their hands; and they lived and reigned with Christ a thousand years. But the rest of the dead lived not again until the thousand years were finished. This is the first resurrection." Before the thousand-year reign of Jesus Christ there will be a further resurrection of those who are Christ's and at the end of the Millennium the unsaved dead will be raised.

In John's visions of the end times, he received messages for seven churches which are interpreted as different periods in church history. The last two churches are Philadelphia and Laodicea, and I believe these two types of churches will both be present when Jesus returns. The Laodicean church was described as lukewarm, indifferent, worldly, though it professed to have Christian faith. The Philadelphia church was pictured as being true to the Word of God and energetic in proclaiming the name of the Lord Jesus Christ. This church received Jesus' promise: "Because thou has kept the word of My patience, I also will keep thee from the hour of temptation, which shall come upon all the world" (3:10). The "hour of temptation," I believe, is to be interpreted as the great tribulation from which believers will be caught away. Left behind will be the "church" which has Christ's name but no part of Him.

There are several reasons that we can imagine for our meeting the Lord in the air. One is it will give the Lord a time of privacy with His followers. The fellowship and worship will be too sacred for alienated beings to see, and so there will be a precious privacy of rejoicing. This meeting will also be a waystop in preparation for proceeding into the presence of God. It seems a necessary pause.

There is another reason. The devil is the "prince of the power of the air" (Eph. 2:2). Satan's headquarters seem to be between earth and the heaven of heavens where God dwells. Perhaps in this conquered territory we will celebrate our final victory with the Captain of our salvation over our greatest enemy. Won't that be glorious!

When we are caught up to meet the Lord, there is going to be a marvelous transformation of our bodies. Paul says, "Behold, I show you a mystery; we shall not all sleep, but we shall all be changed" (1 Cor. 15:51). Everyone will not need to die in order to have his body transfigured. Paul continues, "In the twinkling of an eye, at the last trump . . . we shall be changed" (v. 52). And in Philippians Paul adds: "We look for the Saviour, the Lord Jesus Christ: Who shall change our vile body, that it may be fashioned like unto His glorious body" (Phil. 3:20-21). Think of it! A saint of God suffering with disease will be instantly freed and given a perfect body like Christ's at His return in the skies. And though this change will occur silently and suddenly, imagine the changes on earth.

Perhaps it will take place on a Saturday when a Christian family of four sleeps a little late. They have a leisurely breakfast, then Dad goes out to cut the grass, Mom heads for the grocery store, sister goes swimming, and brother joins the baseball team. That morning the great God of heaven takes a trumpet off the walls of glory and sounds a blast as the Lord descends with a shout. No infidel hears the trumpet nor the shout, but in front of the Christian's house is a lawn mower running with no man to attend it; a cart full of groceries waits for a customer who is no longer hungry; a group of girls in the swimming pool look for their friend who has simply disappeared; and first base is unguarded at the ballpark. All over this world people are missing but they're not lost—the frantic people looking for them are the lost ones!

Rapture Desired

When I was a boy and the preacher talked about the coming of Jesus, it scared me nearly to death. I didn't belong to Jesus then. When I received Jesus as my personal Saviour and came to understand that the second coming of Jesus is "the blessed hope," I realized I was ready for the greatest thrill we can imagine.

Among other changes, the Rapture means a mansion, mysteries unraveled, and multitudes of loving people. It means home and it means happiness. There will be an absence of sin, sorrow, and sickness, and the presence of the greatest people of the ages, beloved people who have gone on before, and Jesus Himself. We can merely begin to imagine the pleasures waiting for us (Ps. 16:11).

When John Glenn, the first American to orbit the earth, returned safely, he was welcomed as a national hero. He was escorted to Washington, and President John Kennedy, speaking for the nation, said, "All America is proud of you." Perhaps you have missed some praise and bouquets of flowers down here, but in heaven you will be honored for your faithful service. Are you ready for that dramatic reentry when God's people, like steel filings drawn to a magnet, will soar up to meet their Saviour?

4

At the Judgment Seat

You're a Christian who is still living when Jesus Christ returns—and meeting Him in the air fills you with jubilation! Right there in the thrilling presence of Jesus and of long-missed friends, all of your sorrows are over and your defeats forgotten. Wrong. Yes, it's true that raptured Christians will be safe in heaven, but many will face deep regrets and shame because they have not lived for God. The Bible teaches that Christians are responsible to Jesus in this life and accountable to Him in the next. After transformation and before glorification comes our examination.

Most banks have a machine into which they toss hundreds of coins of all denominations. When the machine is set into operation, the coins are sorted by size and weight into their proper slots. When we stand before the Judgment Seat all of our deeds will be measured and weighed by the most fair and honest standards ever known.

Actually, there are several judgments taught in the Word of God. There is the judgment of sin which took place at the Cross of Calvary, the daily self-judgment which goes on in the life of the believer, the judgment of nations as recorded in Matthew 25, and the Great White Throne Judgment of all unsaved individuals from the beginning of time. In addition, there is the judgment of Christians' works and awarding of crowns at the Judgment Seat of Christ. This follows the rapture of Christians, and it will be very important to us.

The Christian has already been through one judgment: faith in Christ identified the believer with Christ on the Cross, and the Saviour's death for sin was the believer's death also. Paul assures us, "There is therefore now no condemnation to them who are in Christ Jesus" (Romans 8:1). God dealt with us as sinners when we bowed in repentance at the Cross, and we will never be judged in the future as a sinner.

A second judgment faces us each day as the Holy Spirit confronts our consciences with things in our lives which ought not to be there. We have the choice then of confessing these sins and receiving cleansing, or trying to cover the sins and receiving the chastisement of God. It's one option or the other; Paul says, "If we would judge ourselves, we should not be judged" (1 Cor. 11:31). God thus deals with us not as sinners but as sons.

But there is still a judgment ahead on the basis of our service. Paul tells us: "For we must all appear before the Judgment Seat of Christ, that everyone may receive the things done in his body, according to that he hath done, whether it be good or bad" (2 Cor. 5:10).

The meaning of the "Judgment Seat" for believers is illuminated by the appearance of this Greek word *bema* in other Scriptures. In Acts 18 the Apostle Paul was brought before a Grecian judge on a charge of teaching false doctrines to Jews. The judge wouldn't even listen to a religious case, and he expelled the accusers from his tribunal *bema*.

Another aspect of the Judgment Seat is seen in the *bema* at athletic contests. Winners of various matches came to a platform *bema* in the center of the stadium where an official presented victory wreaths. So the Judgment Seat of Christ is a place of critical discernment and gracious awards.

In a parable, Jesus told His followers when the Judgment Seat examination will take place. "Thou shalt be recompensed [rewarded] at the resurrection of the just" He assured a generous benefactor of poor people (Luke 14:14). And so sometime between the Rapture of the Church and the great Marriage Supper of the Lamb in heaven, there is going to be an examination time, a rectification period when God will bring His people into harmony with Himself and believers with every other believer.

Person At The Judgment

Who is qualified to judge us in that day? It won't be the preacher, or our partner, or our neighbor. Other people cannot look into our motives, so they don't know us well enough to judge us fairly. Jesus warned us about this: "Judge not, that ye be not judged" (Matt. 7:1). We are not given the prerogative of passing judgment upon other believers' behavior because we are so faulty in ourselves.

I heard about a lady who was very critical about other people, and one day she said to her guest: "Would you look at those dirty sheets my neighbor just hung on the line!" Her friend looked out the window and then murmured, "But, my dear, the dirt is on your window, not the sheets." Often we see others through our own distorted vision and become guilty of the very thing we are criticizing.

Neither will we judge ourselves at the *bema*. Until our hearts are cleansed of all sin, we will not know ourselves thoroughly. The Judgment Seat will help us to see ourselves as we really are so that we can be wholly as we should be.

The Lord Jesus Christ will be our judge in that day. He Himself said, "For the Father judgeth no man, but hath committed all judgment unto the Son" (John 5:22). In a sermon to the Athenians, Paul declared that God "hath appointed a day, in which He will judge the world in righteousness by that man whom He hath ordained" (Acts 17:31). Jesus Christ, who knows our innermost thoughts, who loved us enough to die for us, and who wants to make us perfect, will be the Judge.

Procedure At The Judgment

I believe that we will be examined concerning at least five matters at the Judgment Seat. First, we will be examined concerning the quality of our Christian life. A tremendous passage by the Apostle Paul shows where it all begins: "Other foundation can no man lay than that is laid, which is Jesus Christ" (1 Cor. 3:11). Is this where you have begun? There must be a relationship to Jesus Christ in your life on the basis of personal repentance and faith in Him. You must trust totally in Jesus Christ to possess eternal life. The lack of this foundation is the reason some people struggle unsuccessfully to live the Christian life. They are trying to build a skyscraper on a chicken coop foundation. You cannot grow as a Christian until first you have been born into the family of God.

From the moment of your salvation—every believer starts at the same place with the same foundation—you begin choosing materials for building your life. According to their spiritual value, your actions and words may be compared to "gold, silver, precious stones, wood, hay, stubble" (1 Cor. 3:12). There are two kinds of construction material here. Gold, silver, and precious stones are enduring; wood, hay, and stubble are perishable. The first group has intrinsic value, the second group gains value by natural growth. After you make Jesus Christ the foundation of your life, you can erect rooms and stairs and doors with the gold and silver and precious stones supplied by the indwelling Holy Spirit. He will help you build your life if you appoint Him construction boss. Or, you can rummage through the devil's lumberyard for materials. His prices are marked very low, but the cost is far higher in the long run because the material doesn't pass the critical tests.

I believe one of the saddest moments we'll ever face will be to see the kind of Christian life we could have built if we had spent our lives for Jesus Christ, serving Him with loving deeds and selfless endeavors that endure and shine like gold and silver and precious stones. Instead, we will shed bitter tears if we have to look back on a pile of rubble— impure deeds that rot and crumble in the passage of time into eternity.

A second examination at the Judgment Seat concern the words we have spoken. Jesus said, "Every idle word that men shall speak, they shall give account thereof in the day of judgment" (Matt. 12:36). Your words are very important; in fact, they are a good indication of what is in your heart. Jesus said the mouth speaks out of the abundance of the heart. We ought to be very careful of the words we say—because we might hear them again in the presence of Jesus. I have an idea that God is recording every word we say in His supernatural way. Don't you imagine there are going to be embarrassed—and sorrowing—Christians at the Judgment Seat of Christ?

There is power in words to do a great deal of harm or a great deal of good. The Book of Proverbs says, "Death and life are in the power of the tongue" (18:21). You can greatly enhance the ministry of another Christian, you can be a tremendous blessing by the words you use, or your words can spread poison like the bite of a deadly serpent. James said the tongue is set on fire by hell—how much destruction fire can cause! But, "The tongue of the wise useth knowledge aright" (Prov. 15:2).

Further, we will be examined at the Judgment Seat concerning our faithfulness to Christ. Jesus told a story to illustrate this truth. He said His kingdom can be compared to a man going to a far country, who first gathered his servants and distributed money among them to be invested until he returned. One servant received five talents, another two, and the third a single talent, each portion corresponding to the servant's ability to use the money. The master went away, and the servants went to work—at least two did.

The first took advantage of the opportunities he was given and earned five more talents. The second was equally diligent and he doubled his two talents. The third man fearfully—or lazily—buried his talent instead of putting it to work. When the master returned for an accounting, each of the two men who used and doubled his legacy heard the master say, "Well done, good and faithful servant; thou hast been faithful over a few things, I will make thee ruler over many things" (Matt. 25:23).

Our Saviour teaches here that every Christian will be judged by his faithfulness in using the gifts God has given him. Remember that your gifts may not be my gifts, but we all have some to be used for God's glory.

One of the serious problems of Christians is our unfaithfulness to the opportunities God has given us. Some Christians are Sunday School teachers; are you faithful to that responsibility? Some sing in the choir; are you committed to that ministry? God has given me the privilege of preaching the Gospel, and I will render an account to Him of my faithfulness.

Won't it be tragic to stand before our wonderful Saviour and hear: "I gave you an ability to serve Me in a particular way and time, and you squandered it"? Perhaps He will add, "Didn't you love Me enough to obey when I needed you?" What shame we will feel!

I believe we will also be judged concerning our attitude and conduct toward other believers. A searching passage in Romans 14 goes deep into the experience of some of us. Paul writes: "One believeth that he may eat all things: another, who is weak, eateth herbs. Let not him that eateth despise him that eateth not; and let not him which eateth not judge him that eateth: for God hath received him. Who art thou that judgest another man's servant? To his own master he standeth or falleth" (vv. 2-4).

Paul says a Christian has no right to condemn another Christian for debatable practices. The Bible is clear in prohibiting certain acts which are sinful, but it leaves much conduct as a matter between the individual and his Lord.

One of the ugliest and most destructive habits in Christians is the attitude of criticizing and condemning other Christians. Christians are not accountable to one another, though we are responsible to *help* other Christians when they commit evident sin. If you see something in the life of a believer which you believe is harmful, ask God to help him, for to his *Master* the Christian stands or falls. How can there be an atmosphere of love in God's house when our conversation is filled with critical gossip of one another? In many churches there are so many petty quarrels going on that it is amazing the Spirit of God breaks through the animosity to save anyone.

I want to warn Christians who refuse to fellowship with another believer that their bitterness and arrogance will be exposed at the Judgment Seat of Christ. If you don't straighten out the matter down here, our holy Saviour will fix it up there—and I think it will be much more painful then.

Not only will our behavior be examined at the *bema*, but our inner motives will be scrutinized. Jesus indicated this after observing people contribute money in the temple.

In Bible days the offering box for the poor had a

tapering funnel, like a horn, to catch contributions dropped into the box. Apparently some hypocrites had become expert in flinging tiny coins at the funnel opening in a way that resounded their clang throughout the area, calling attention to their gift. But Jesus said public recognition was the only reward these donors would gain because their motives were self-centered. "Take heed that ye do not your alms before men to be seen by them;" Jesus warned his disciples, "Otherwise ye have no reward of your Father which is in heaven" (Matt. 6:1).

I'd like you to examine yourself now as to why you do helpful things for others and invest your efforts in church work. Is it for the glory of the Lord Jesus Christ, or for personal recognition? I know a lady whose name was accidently left off the workers' list in Vacation Bible School, and she was so angry she stayed away from church for two years. It's obvious whom she was serving!

At the Judgment Seat you will be examined concerning why you sang in the choir or taught Sunday School or served on a committee, and the wrong motive will rob that action of any lasting value for you or God.

Yes, God will wipe away all tears from our eyes, we're told. That will be a blessing, but a greater blessing will be to smile as you hear, "Well done, good and faithful servant."

Purpose For The Judgment

"There ain't no justice," some people complain, and they're often right about this world's justice. But things will be different at the Judgment Seat of Christ. "The Lord . . . will bring to light the hidden things of darkness, and will make manifest the counsels of the hearts: and then shall every man have praise of God" (1 Cor. 4:5). Many things will be brought to light that will rectify distortions on earth: misunderstood motives, misquoted individuals, slandered Christians, and slighted service. These inequities are going to be made right.

I know some Christians who give unselfishly of their time and energy to work in the church, and they're not rewarded down here. All of that is going to be spotlighted at the Judgment Seat of Christ, and there are going to be some surprise shifts in the rankings. Some well-known Christians who expect a place of honor close to Jesus will discover they haven't qualified for that position. And others who serve in obscurity here will be brought forward when they receive the true evaluation of the all-seeing Judge.

A beautiful part of the judgment will be the giving of rewards. Rewards—aren't they vain and carnal? Not when Jesus gives them!

Jesus says: "Behold, I come quickly; and my reward is with me, to give every man according as his work shall be" (Rev. 22:12). And David wrote: "There is a reward for the righteous" (Ps. 58:11). Even a cup of cold water given in the name of a disciple will receive a reward, Jesus promised (Matt. 10:42).

But these rewards are different from most earthly honors. In fact, if you do something for the purpose of receiving God's reward, you've already cancelled it because your motive was wrong. Heavenly rewards will be genuinely merited by the recipients, but in many cases they will be surprises!

In the Greek New Testament there are two words for crown: *diadema,* the royal crown of the king;

and *stephanos*, which means the victor's crown or laurel wreath. Several victor's wreaths await their winners at the Judgment Seat. There is the crown of self-control mentioned in 1 Corinthians 9:25; the crown of life in James 1:12; and the soul-winners crown in 1 Thessalonians 2:19. There are rewards and crowns for everything done in Jesus' name, producing great joy.

Can you imagine the exultation that will be experienced by those who receive the praise of God? Our Father is appreciative of His children's faithfulness, and He will not forget. It doesn't matter whether other humans congratulate you or not; it doesn't matter whether others understand you or not, if you can stand at the Judgment Seat of Christ and hear the Lord say, "My child, you did your best for Me. Now I will honor you." In that moment we'll rejoice over everything we did for His sake.

There is one other reason for the Judgment Seat, I believe. In Ephesians 5:27 we read that the Lord is going to present His church without spot or wrinkle to its glorious destiny in eternity. I confess that there are some wrinkles and spots in my life which aren't likely to be removed before I stand at the Judgment Seat of Christ. But there every stain and flaw of my personality will vanish at the touch of Christ, and I will be just exactly what He wants me to be.

The Apostle John urges: "Little children, abide in Him; that, when He shall appear, we may have confidence, and not be ashamed before Him at His coming" (1 John 2:28). Will you have that confidence and delight? You will if you build your life by heaven's construction code.

5

Here Comes
the Bridegroom!

Can you recall the details of the most beautiful wedding you ever attended? Do you remember the glowing face of the bride? Or the beaming pride of the groom? Maybe the setting was unforgettable, or the exchanged vows soul-stirring. Whether elaborate or simple, the reverent joining of two lives is an exalted and unique experience.

Having seen or participated in a lovely wedding, you have a small idea of the great event awaiting Christians: the Marriage Supper of the Lamb. Here is a partial description of the event given in Revelation 19:7-9.

"Let us be glad and rejoice, and give honor to Him: for the Marriage of the Lamb is come, and His wife hath made herself ready. And to her was granted that she should be arrayed in fine linen, clean and white: for the fine linen is the righteousness of the saints. And he saith unto me, Write, Blessed are they which are called unto the Marriage

Supper of the Lamb. And he saith unto me, These are the true sayings of God."

The scene is too magnificent to take in all at once, but looking at some comparisons within our present experience will deepen our understanding.

The Church of Jesus Christ, made up of all true believers in Him, is like a temple being built for the glory of God. The foundation is Christ, and the whole structure reflects the splendor of a Master Architect. More intricately, the Church is likened to a healthy human body, coordinating its actions to serve one purpose. The third analogy is the Church as a bride, promised to the heavenly Bridegroom and destined for a divine marriage. Being the "body" of Christ who is "head", reminds us of the nearness of Jesus to His Church; being the bride assures us of the dearness of the Church to Him.

In the Old Testament, we are told that Jehovah was the great Husband of God's people, Israel, "As the bridegroom rejoiceth over the bride, so shall thy God rejoice over thee." "Thy Maker is thine Husband; the Lord of hosts is His name" (Isa. 62:5; 54:5). In the New Testament we learn that the Church is the bride and wife of Jesus, who proved His love by dying for her salvation (Eph. 5:25). One of these days when the bride is ready— when all those whom Jesus has called have answered—the bride of our Lord will meet Him in the air and proceed to the festive marriage banquet!

The Marriage Supper of the Lamb speaks to us of the full spiritual union of the Church with Jesus Christ. It reminds us of the intimate communion and joy and fidelity which ought to exist between God's people and God's Son.

Procuring the Bride

Early in Jesus' ministry on earth, He began to depict the love relationship between Himself and His followers. When he was asked why His disciples were not fasting like the followers of other religious leaders, Jesus said, "Can the children of the bridechamber mourn, as long as the Bridegroom is with them? But the days will come when the Bridegroom shall be taken from them, and then shall they fast" (Matt. 9:15). Jesus identified Himself as a Bridegroom who was going away for a period of time and then would return.

In Jesus' day there were two ceremonies in a marriage, the first known as espousal, which can be compared to our modern engagement period. The parents of the man and woman would announce their intentions for the couple to be married, and a waiting period of indefinite length would permit all preparations to be made and their pledge confirmed. The wedding celebration completed formal union of marriage. The Apostle Paul referred to this custom when he wrote: "I am jealous over you with godly jealousy: for I have espoused you to one husband, that I may present you as a chaste virgin to Christ" (2 Cor. 11:2).

When Jesus Christ saves a soul, that person becomes a part of the bride of Jesus Christ, entering an engagement period. It has been more than 1,900 years since the Bridegroom left for heaven, and we are awaiting His return and the ultimate marriage banquet.

When a young couple gets married today, the bride is the center of attraction. She's the one pictured in the newspaper, the one honored at parties, and the one admired at the wedding. Most grooms could be barefooted without causing a stir. Maybe all that attention to the bride helps the bridegroom appreciate her more, as he should.

In Bible days the center of attraction was the bridegroom. Parties heralded the groom's wedding, and his friends gathered to escort him to the house of his bride and on to the new residence of the couple. Perhaps the man was honored because the success of the marriage depended so greatly on his leadership and fidelity. This is uniquely true of the marriage celebrating the union of Christ with His church.

Surprisingly, the Old Testament contains several illustrations of this divine relationship. One is of the first bride, Eve, whom God made from a rib taken from the side of Adam. It was from the wounded side of our Lord that His blood poured forth to give life to the Church.

Another bride which illustrates this truth is Rebekah. She heard about Isaac, her prospective groom, from a servant who informed her of the greatness of his master. Rebekah was willing to leave her country and go to Isaac because she loved him though she had never seen him.

The Church, like Rebekah, has been procured and is awaiting the Marriage Day.

Preparing the Bride

Our Scripture says that "His wife hath made herself ready" (Rev. 19:7). When did that take place? I believe this happens at the Judgment Seat of Christ where all of the blemishes of the believers are eliminated and the Church becomes a fitting bride for the Son of God. Three steps are involved in this preparation.

First, we look at the wedding garments. "And to her was granted that she should be arrayed in fine linen, clean and white: for the fine linen is the righteousness of saints" (v. 8). In Bible days two garments customarily were worn: an inner cloak known as the tunic, an outer robe, perhaps more beautiful, called a toga. Similarly, two garments may be seen in the proper preparation of the bride for her Lord.

The inner garment of fine linen is provided by the Groom: it is His righteousness imputed to us. You and I have no goodness of our own to qualify us for heaven. Isaiah gives us God's estimate of our flawed efforts: "All of our righteousnesses are as filthy rags" (64:6). We may be "good" in human perspective, but we don't meet God's perfect standard. But the Apostle Paul tells us about another righteousness: it is Christ's own perfection given or imputed to believers. It is Christ's goodness that makes His bride holy and acceptable to God.

Jesus told a parable in Matthew 22 that dramatizes the importance of this wedding garment. Many guests were invited to a wedding banquet and were provided with a special robe as they entered. The king arrived to join the festivities and as he circulated among the guests he encountered one who had no wedding garment. The only reason for such a deficiency would be the visitor's preference for his own apparel. It wasn't adequate; he was expelled from the banquet. Celebrants at the Marriage Supper of the Lamb must have Jesus' robe of righteousness.

The typical outer garment or toga was usually attractive in its ornamentation. This garment represents the wearer's acts and words that glorify God. Our selfless service to God will be evident at the Marriage Supper.

In ancient days the bride was expected to present a valuable gift, a dowry, to the groom. That custom will be reenacted at the Marriage Supper of Christ (Rev. 4:4-11).

Here we see the twenty-four elders who represent God's people, sitting upon thrones, garbed in the white raiment of Christ's righteousness and wearing crowns of gold. "The four and twenty elders fall down before Him that sat on the throne, and worship Him that liveth for ever and ever, and cast their crowns before the throne, saying, Thou art worthy, O Lord" (vv. 10-11).

When we go to that great marriage supper and we are rewarded for the things we have done for the Lord Jesus Christ, we will cherish the crowns for the honor they will accord Him when we worshipfully place them at His feet. They will be our wedding gift to the Groom!

Notice in Revelation 19:9 that there will be some guests at the wedding. "And he saith unto me, Write, Blessed are they which are called unto the marriage supper of the Lamb." Since no bride is invited to her own wedding, these must be special guests. I believe they will be the Old Testament saints—not a part of the Church in the New Testament sense of the word—who will be invited as the friends of the Bridegroom.

You recall that John the Baptist said, "He that hath the bride is the bridegroom: but the friend of the bridegroom, which standeth and heareth him, rejoiceth greatly because of the bridegroom's voice" (John 3:29). John the Baptist was the "friend" of

Jesus who pointed people to the Bridegroom. The Old Testament saints have already entered eternity, and they will be honored guests at the Marriage Supper. The prophets and patriots and priests and saints of all callings from pre-Christian times will greet the bride and the Groom and be seated at the banquet table to rejoice together. All is ready for presenting the bride.

Presenting the Bride

When you think about a perfect marriage, what qualities do you see? I see, first of all, purity. In Ephesians 5:27 we read that Christ "will present it to Himself a glorious church, not having spot, or wrinkle." Miraculously, beautifully, all imperfections have been exchanged for moral purity.

Marriage brings together two and makes them one. The bride will be in adoring submission to the love-impelled Groom. In human phraseology, the Bridegroom has written a love song to his bride. It is the Song of Solomon in eight stanzas in the Old Testament. The theme of the song is: "My beloved is mine and I am His." No earthly partnership compares with the harmony and bliss of this heavenly marriage.

And there will be permanence, for this union will not be vulnerable to misunderstandings, bitterness, and alienation. It will be the "perfect match," and subsequent life will only deepen the relationship—forever.

In the Rapture Jesus will catch us up, at the Judgment Seat He will clean us up, and at the Marriage Supper He will cheer us up! Then will follow a thousand-year honeymoon during Jesus' millennial rule.

Are you going to be there? The Bible invites you; our Saviour has sent you a written invitation, and He waits for your response if you have not yet answered.

Jesus told another parable about this Marriage Supper. He said ten virgins made preparations for the coming of the bridegroom, but only five of them secured enough oil to keep their lamps burning through the night in case the bridegroom was delayed (Matt. 25:1-12). At midnight the call was heard: "Here comes the bridegroom." Those who had the light of life went out to meet the bridegroom and proceeded to the wedding supper. Those who were not ready came late to the banquet hall and knocked at the door, but the bridegroom refused them, saying, "I do not know you."

Will you be outside when the door to the Marriage Supper is shut? God now gives you another chance to be saved. The Bridegroom is coming; He invites all who hear to His supper, and to share in His glory.

6

Tribulation
on the Earth

Looking around on a beautiful spring morning, the poet Robert Browning exulted: "The lark's on the wing / The snail's on the thorn / God's in His heaven / All's right with the world." But what would a sensitive poet see in the wintertime of human history, when God is celebrating His Son's marriage in heaven and allowing Satan to take over the world?

We don't have to guess, because the Scriptures depict the scene on earth after Christ has taken His bride to heaven. The disorder, suffering, and fear will exceed anything the world has ever seen.

The Old Testament prophets gave the first description of these terrible days. From their perspective, we see God's punishing judgment descending on the world which has rejected Him. Isaiah wrote: "Howl ye; for the day of the Lord is at hand; it shall come as a destruction from the Almighty. . . . Behold, the day of the Lord cometh, cruel both with wrath and fierce anger, to lay the land desolate: and He shall destroy the sinners thereof out of it. . . . And I will punish the world for their evil, and the wicked for their iniquity; and I will cause the arrogancy of the proud to cease, and will lay low the haughtiness of the terrible" (13:6, 9, 11).

The prophet Joel adds to the picture: "Alas for the day! For the day of the Lord is at hand, and as a destruction from the Almighty shall it come. . . . Blow the trumpet in Zion, and sound an alarm in My holy mountain. Let all the inhabitants of the land tremble; for the day of the Lord cometh, for it is nigh at hand; a day of darkness and of gloominess, a day of clouds and thick darkness, as the morning spread upon the mountains; a great people and a strong; there hath not been ever the like, neither shall be any more after it, even to the years of many generations" (Joel 1:15; 2:1-2).

Israel's ancient prophets received a glimpse of earth's last days, and called it the "day of the Lord," the "day of darkness," the "day of vengeance," and the "day of Jacob's trouble" because Jacob's descendants would find themselves in the midst of the calamities.

New Testament writers were given many more details of earth's death struggles. Jesus Himself warned, "Then shall be great tribulation, such as was not since the beginning of the world to this time, no, nor ever shall be" (Matt. 24:21). Conditions will be so destructive, Jesus added, that no one would survive unless God intervenes, which He will do.

The fullest description of the tribulation period appears in the Book of Revelation, chapters 6 through 19. First, let's look at a key number in these chapters.

In Revelation 11:2 we read the time period of "42 months"; in 12:6 "one thousand two hundred and threescore (1,260) days"; and in 12:14 "a time and times, and half a time" (or three and one-half). Each of these figures corresponds to three and one-half years—a significant period for several events. Before investigating the events, we go back to Daniel to examine a crucial prophecy.

The angel Gabriel came to Daniel and announced: "Seventy weeks are determined upon thy people and upon thy holy city, to finish the transgression, and to make an end of sins, and to make reconciliation for iniquity, and to bring in everlasting righteousness, and to seal up the vision and prophecy, and to anoint the most Holy" (9:24).

Daniel was in Babylon at the time of this vision, longing for the return of his captive people to their holy city, Jerusalem. Here the angel tells Daniel that within a period of 70 weeks the Jews would return to Jerusalem, an atonement for sin would be made, everlasting righteousness would begin, and Israel's Messiah would be anointed! These staggering promises can be understood only as the "seventy weeks" is properly interpreted.

In Leviticus 25 a "week" is taken to mean seven years instead of seven days. "Seventy weeks" then can mean "seventy sevens" of years, or 490 years. Many Bible commentators agree on this interpretation, and it is supported by the rest of the prophecy.

"Know therefore and understand, that from the going forth of the commandment to restore and to build Jerusalem unto the Messiah the Prince shall be seven weeks, and threescore and two weeks: the street shall be built again, and the wall, even in troublous times. And after threescore and two weeks shall Messiah be cut off, but not for Himself: and the people of the prince that shall come shall destroy the city and the sanctuary; and the end thereof shall be with a flood, and unto the end of the war desolations are determined" (Dan. 9:25-26).

The fulfillment of these prophecies can be clearly traced. Nehemiah tells when King Artaxerxes authorized him to return to Jerusalem and rebuild its walls. And the Gospel books record the death or "cutting off" of the Messiah.

An English lawyer, Robert Anderson, carefully computed the time interval between the edict of Artaxerxes and the crucifixion of Christ and found it to be 483 years, or 69 "weeks" of years. This leaves one more "week" in the 70 designated to establish a righteous king over the earth. The rest of the prophecy gives more light.

"And he shall confirm"—referring to "the prince of the people who shall come" in verse 26—"the covenant with many for one week, and in the midst of the week he shall cause the sacrifice and oblation to cease, and for the overspreading of abominations he shall make it desolate even until the consummation, and that determined shall be poured upon the desolate" (v. 27).

These events of the "seventieth week of Daniel" have never taken place, and so we are led to conclude that there is a time gap between the events of verses 26 and 27, a gap that continues to this day. The reasons for this interpretation are shown in the Scriptures.

When Jesus came to the world the first time, He offered Himself to the Jews as their long-awaited King, though He wanted acceptance as their spiritual Ruler, not political. Israel rejected His claims and crucified Him, revealing their spiritual rebellion against God. At that time God's prophetic clock for the Jewish nation stopped ticking, and another clock recording the "times of the Gentiles" began ticking. God set aside the Jewish nation, as Paul explains in Romans 11, to send the Gospel of salvation to the Gentile nations in the "age of grace" or free salvation. We are living in that era.

But one of these days the clock marking the Gentiles' progress is going to stop, and God will start the Jews' historical clock again to run for seven years till the end. The Gentiles' great opportunity for salvation ends when Christ raptures His church. Then follows the "seventieth week" that will "finish the transgression" in an unprecedented torrent of tribulations (Dan 9:24).

As God's prophetic timepiece for the Jewish nation resumes ticking, a political leader makes a treaty with Israel for a seven-year period (9:27). But in the middle of the treaty period he breaks the covenant and halts the Jews' temple sacrifices. Half of seven years is three and a half years, or 42 months, or 1,260 days—remember those figures? They mark the duration of tumult for the whole earth recorded in Revelation. The prince of Daniel 9:26-27 who desecrates the temple worship is the world leader of Revelation 11 and 12 who rules the Gentile Tribulation. I want to point out three particularly important things about the coming Great Tribulation.

Chaos Of The Tribulation

Since the Rapture of the Church will be sudden and secret, there will be no time to leave farewell notes or good-byes. In a twinkling of an eye God's people will be caught up and there will be sudden disappearances all over the world. Some husbands will awaken to discover that their wives are not by their side. Businesses will be stripped of leaders and dependable workers. The halls of Congress will miss many men of integrity and morality. Can you imagine the consternation on earth, the turmoil and chaos which will take place when every born-again child of God is taken out of this world?

Jesus declared that His Church is the salt of the earth and the moral light that keeps the world from going rotten. We Christians can take no personal credit for this; it is the result of the Holy Spirit's life in us. But one of these days that salt is going to be taken away, and that light will be withdrawn, plunging the world into spiritual darkness and moral corruption. Christians may not be especially noticed by their fellowmen now, but they will be grievously missed when they're gone.

Chaos will also spread from the series of judgments sent from heaven. The Book of Revelation describes seven seal judgments and three bowl judgments being poured on the earth. Why will God release these searing judgments?

God has decreed that the world will suffer for its rejection of His Son and reception of Satan's evil Antichrist. Most of the world has had no use for the Son of God, the only truly good Man in history. They scorn the claim that He died because of His love for them, and repudiate the idea that their misdeeds deserve death. Their rejection of the good news of salvation becomes their greatest sin.

Some people have asked me if many unbelievers will trust in Christ after the Christians are taken away and the Gospel is recalled by multitudes who heard it and did not respond. While this is a question about which many devout believers differ, I have a scriptural answer that persuades me of the feeble prospects for such a hope.

This answer is in Paul's description of the reaction of God-rejectors to the amazing achievements of the Antichrist. "They received not the love of the truth, that they might be saved. And for this cause God shall send them strong delusion, that they should believe a lie: that they all might be damned who believed not the truth, but had pleasure in unrighteousness" (2 Thes. 2:10-12).

Does that sound like a second chance to get right with God? It sounds more like a death sentence. We know people who have repentantly turned to God when suffering adverse circumstances, but more are inclined to rage against God. As the terrors of the Tribulation heighten, many will beg the rocks and the mountains to fall upon them to escape further torment (Rev. 6:16). The man-made utopia will be unbearable.

Characteristics Of The Tribulation

Scripture tells us about the political, economic, and religious characteristics of Antichrist's kingdom. We learn a great deal just by the names given to the Antichrist. Paul calls him "the man of sin," "the son of perdition," and "the wicked one" (2 Thes. 2:3, 8). We will look at this man more closely in a separate study, but let's consider briefly how the world is preparing the way for this leader.

Travel, communications, and trade are making our world smaller and smaller—and our problems larger and larger. National leaders foresee the day when a superstatesman will be needed, a man brilliant and influential enough to forge peace between the nations. His superhuman ability will gain the rulership of the world.

The idea of a world government is not new. Plato wrote about his ideal world government 25 centuries ago. Today leading politicians in America and Europe endorse a world government that will establish peace and coordinate the endeavors of all nations. Mankind will welcome this political messiah when he appears on the scene.

Economically, the Antichrist will rule commerce and finances with a totalitarian fist. He that controls money controls life and death, and the Antichrist will not let such power out of his hands. Of course, he will promise relief to the underprivileged, support to the hard-working middle class, and guidance to the capitalists. He will outdo the socialist planners in promising something for everyone, and too late everyone will discover they have surrendered their freedom for bread, their inner peace for outward regimentation.

We already see some of the curses of totalitarianism in Communist countries. They have peace—with standing armies that assure no one will step out of line. They feed all the people—except those marked for starvation in the concentration camps. For a graphic look at the totalitarian empire of the future, read George Orwell's chilling book, *1984*. Follow that with the last three verses of Revelation 13—and ask yourself if that's the kind of government you want.

Perhaps you wouldn't expect the Antichrist to tolerate religion in his kingdom—I assure you there will be plenty of religion. One of Antichrist's early acts will be to make a peace treaty with the Jewish people that will restore their right to worship according to their desires. That's the meaning of Daniel 9:27—"He shall confirm the covenant with many for one week," to rebuild that temple which the Antichrist will later profane. The Jews, the most persecuted and plundered people on earth, will honor the Antichrist for solving the Mideast crises. Other religions will move toward unity by emphasizing their similarities and discarding their differences.

The Antichrist will reveal his true nature in the middle of the tribulation period when he orders temple sacrifices to cease and everyone to worship him. With death their only alternative, most people will choose to worship Satan's ambassador!

A remarkable thing will occur during this time: 144,000 Jews will be converted to preach the Gospel of the kingdom to the ends of the earth! They will not have much time, and they will be slain for opposing the Antichrist, but they will carry the Good News to those who have not had the opportunity to hear.

We read about these fearless evangelists in Revelation 7. They die for Christ under the sword of the Antichrist, but they lead many souls to heaven from various peoples of earth. They too will seal their faith with their own blood. Such will be religion in the Tribulation.

Conclusion Of The Tribulation

How will it all end? We will only summarize it at

this point by saying the Great Tribulation will conclude with the greatest war of all time.

In Revelation 16, we read: "For they are the spirits of devils, working miracles, which go forth unto the kings of the earth and of the whole world, to gather them to the battle of that great day of God Almighty. . . . And He gathered them together into a place called in the Hebrew tongue Armageddon" (vv. 14, 16).

Megiddo was a hilltop city in northwest Israel overlooking a wide, flat plain stretching south toward Jerusalem and north toward Syria. The armies of the ancient Egyptians and Assyrians clashed here, as well as more recent armies of the French and British. In peacetime it is the fertile Valley of Esdraelon. Its strategic position and wide expanse make it the site of the world's last great conflict. Russia will advance from the north, Oriental armies from the east, and a coalition of nations under the Antichrist from Europe to attack Jerusalem and annihilate the Jewish people. Will it be another slaughter like the Nazi obliteration of the Warsaw ghetto?

Turn to Revelation 19 for the answer. "And I saw heaven opened, and behold a white horse; and He that sat upon him was called Faithful and True, and in righteousness He doth judge and make war. . . . And the armies which were in heaven followed Him upon white horses, clothed in fine linen, white and clean. And out of His mouth goeth a sharp sword, that with it He should smite the nations: and He shall rule them with a rod of iron (vv. 11, 14-15). That's the victory scene: end of Antichrist; end of Tribulation.

Some Christians believe the Rapture will not

occur soon enough to spare them the tribulations of the Antichrist. There are several Scriptures that convince me Christians will not go through the Great Tribulation.

One says: "Ye turned to God from idols to serve the living and true God, and to wait for His Son from heaven whom He raised from the dead, even Jesus, which delivered us from the wrath to come" (1 Thes. 1:9-10). God will deliver us from this wrath to come.

In another Scripture Jesus promises the Philadelphian church: "I also will keep thee from the hour of temptation, which shall come upon all the world" (Rev. 3:10).

A new insight into similar passages in Revelation clinched the conviction for me. Seven times at the conclusion of Jesus' messages to the churches He repeats: "He that hath an ear to hear, let him hear what the Spirit saith to the churches." After this we see no mention of the Church on the earth until it comes back with Jesus, described in Revelation 19. But in the midst of these chapters which depict the Tribulation on earth, a familiar warning appears: "If any man have an ear, let him hear" (13:9). If *who* hears? "Any man." Not the *church,* as in the third chapter, *because the churches aren't there* to receive the warning! They are in heaven with Jesus during the Tribulation havoc.

I am willing to suffer and die for Jesus during the Tribulation—but that is not His plan. Praise God for His great salvation!

7

Rise and Fall
of the Antichrist

We Christians know Christ and His characteristics —would we recognize His great enemy, the Antichrist, if we saw him? Our embarrassing failures in the past indicate that attempts to identify the Antichrist are reckless and harmful.

Some early Christians, for example, were convinced that Nero was the Antichrist. In this century Benito Mussolini was labeled the Antichrist by some Christian leaders when he mobilized Italy and formed the Rome-Berlin alliance. In recent years Christian publications have speculated on the possibility that U.S. diplomat Henry Kissinger is the Antichrist. This kind of sensational conjecture causes non-Christians to ridicule Bible prophecy.

The truth is that many political leaders have shown some of the characteristics of the Antichrist, but none has been the epitome of evil who unmistakably represents Satan on earth. According to my understanding of Paul's prophecy, Antichrist's identity will not be known until *after* the Rapture of the Church.

"Now we beseech you, brethren, by the coming of our Lord Jesus Christ, and by our gathering together unto Him, that ye be not soon shaken in mind, or be troubled, neither by spirit, nor by word, nor by letter as from us, as that the day of Christ is at hand. Let no man deceive you by any means: for that day shall not come, except there come a falling away first, and that man of sin be revealed, the son of perdition; who opposeth and exalteth himself above all that is called God, or that is worshiped; so that he as God sitteth in the temple of God, shewing himself that he is God. Remember ye not, that, when I was with you, I told you these things? And now ye know what withholdeth that he might be revealed in his time. For the mystery of iniquity doth already work: only He who now letteth [restraineth] will let until He be taken out of the way. And then shall that wicked one be revealed, whom the Lord shall consume with the spirit of His mouth, and shall destroy with the brightness of His coming" (2 Thes. 2:1-8).

It is important to recognize that there has been a titanic struggle between forces of good and evil all through human history. In Genesis 3:15 we see the beginning of the struggle after Adam and Eve's first sin. God declared He would put enmity between the seed of the serpent and the seed of the woman, and continual warfare has resulted. The culmination of everything good and honorable on earth was Jesus Christ, the divine Son of God. The culmination of all that is evil and destructive on earth will be the brilliant and barbarous personality called Antichrist. There will be only one Antichrist, but Satan's hatred has raged in many little "anti-christs" throughout history. The Bible helps us discern between the little ones and the ultimate one.

His Description

The Apostle John tells about the rise of antichristian forces in New Testament days. "And every spirit that confesseth not that Jesus Christ is come in the flesh is not of God: and this is that spirit of antichrist, which ye have heard that it should come, and even now already is it in the world. . . . As ye have heard that Antichrist shall come, even now are there many antichrists" (1 John 2:18; 4:3).

Paul gives us further discernment in the passage we've already read. "That day [day of the Lord] shall not come, except there come a falling away first, and that man of sin be revealed . . . and now ye know what withholdeth that he might be revealed in his time. For the mystery of iniquity doth already work: only He who now letteth [withholdeth or restraineth] will let, until He be taken out of the way" (2 Thes. 2:3, 6-7).

Some Bible scholars have interpreted that "falling away" as the departing of the Church in the Rapture. I believe it refers to the departing of nominal Christians from the faith, but we see here a second sign that the Church will be raptured before the Antichrist is revealed.

The Antichrist will not appear on the world's stage until a restraining influence is removed. Some have interpreted the restrainer to be civil government which will resist takeover by this mighty dictator. But constitutional government will be no obstacle to a supernaturally empowered tyrant.

Divine power is the only force that can restrain Satan, so I believe this "withholder" is the Spirit of God.

We read in Isaiah 59:19 that it is the Spirit of the Lord who will lift up a standard against the enemy. Our civilization worldwide seems to be moving on a flood tide of evil. Yet something keeps turning back the surging currents that threaten to break out of control. I believe this is the presence of the Holy Spirit dwelling in born-again believers. We are counteracting evil by the power of the Spirit in us, and when we leave the earth at the Rapture the supernatural restraining influence will also leave, opening the floodgates for the Antichrist.

We have noted that the Antichrist is called the "man of sin." Not the "man of mistakes" or "weak character" or "bad companions," but man of *sin*. Revelation 13:18 gives a mysterious clue to this man in the form of a number: 666.

Throughout Scripture the number seven is seen as the number of perfection or completion. The number six is often linked with man whose main spiritual trait is failure. So three sixes are appropriate for this trinity of imperfection. He will be the epitome of man's failure and sin.

The Antichrist is also called the "son of perdition" or destruction. This term is both a description and a destination. Some commentators have linked the Antichrist to Judas Iscariot who is also called the "son of perdition" (John 17:12). Judas did yield himself to the devil and betray Jesus Christ. Then he committed suicide and "went to his own place." In Revelation 13 the Antichrist "beast" is depicted as ascending out of the bottomless pit, and some Bible interpreters conclude that the Antichrist will be Judas Iscariot reincarnated. This is interesting speculation, but no one can say with finality who the Antichrist will be.

His third title is "that wicked one" which might be translated "that lawless one." Lawlessness is total disregard for law, whether God's law or man's.

The Western nations constructed their legal systems on the moral authority of God and His righteous commandments. But belief in the existence of God has been crumbling in all areas of Western society. Disorder and meaninglessness have infiltrated art, music, philosophy, and even science. Many intellectual leaders can see no God behind life, and therefore no authority for moral standards. Such people will be a pushover for the "lawless one" and his creed: "Do whatever makes you feel good." This philosophy has already gone a long way toward replacing the Ten Commandments.

We find other significant descriptions of the Antichrist in Daniel and Revelation: "the little horn"; "the king of fierce countenance"; "the prince of the people that shall come"; the rider "on a white horse" who goes forth to conquer; and a "beast out of the earth" and "out of the sea." All of these signify activities and powers which we will investigate further. Names in Scripture hold special meaning, even for the Antichrist.

His Dominion

The Bible clearly informs us that this world is under the dominion of Satan. John tells us: "The whole world lieth in wickedness" (1 John 5:19). That is a long way from God's original plan.

When God created the earth, His crowning masterpiece was mankind, fashioned on the sixth day. Adam and Eve were the summit of God's designing wisdom and power.

God said to this final creation: "I'm giving you all of this creation, the animals, birds of the air, and the fish of the sea. You are to have dominion over them and use them for your benefit."

But man deliberately sinned against God and automatically lost his dominion over the earth. The new ruler was Satan, the prince of this world by right of conquest over man. Consequently Paul calls Satan the "prince of the power of the air" (Eph. 2:2) and the "god of this world" (2 Cor. 4:4).

The devil is in charge of worldly governments, and so he could offer Jesus the kingdoms of this world if Jesus would worship him. Jesus refused the offer, of course, choosing instead the way of the Cross and redemption of sinners from the clutches of the devil. By His faithfulness, Jesus insured the future transfer of power when "the kingdoms of this world are become the kingdoms of our Lord, and of His Christ" (Rev. 11:15).

Whereas Jesus refused the devil's offer, the Antichrist will accept it. He will then rule over all nations—under Satan's supervision, of course. I believe His authority will be exerted through a coalition of nations in Europe. The basis for this interpretation is a vision of Daniel recorded in chapter 7.

This vision portrays four beasts that are revealed to be four great empires. By comparison with the revelation to Daniel in chapter 2, we see that the beasts represent Babylon, Medo-Persia, Greece, and Rome. Whereas the earlier vision had a statue of a man with ten toes, the fourth beast here has ten horns.

As Daniel watched the horns, "there came up among them another little horn, before whom there were three of the first horns plucked up by the roots; and, behold, in this horn were eyes like the eyes of man, and a mouth speaking great things" (7:8).

In Revelation 13 we see a beast with these characteristics making war against "the saints"—followers of God, and speaking great blasphemies against God. I believe this little horn is the Antichrist, rising to power from the area of the old Roman Empire, and persuading the peoples of the world that he has the answer to their urgent problems.

Even today people are talking about the growing need for leaders who can resolve the problems of our cities, of the environment, and of international tensions. The Antichrist will convince the statesmen of the world that he has the solution, and I believe that we are getting ready now for a world government led by the Antichrist.

His Designs

We are completely safe in gauging the designs of the Antichrist on the basis of the known designs of the devil. What is the goal of the devil? We see it in Isaiah 14:12-14.

"How are thou fallen from heaven, O Lucifer . . . how are thou cut down to the ground. . . . For thou hast said in thine heart, I will ascend into heaven, I will exalt my throne above the stars of God . . . I will be like the most High."

Satan wants to be worshiped, and his human

commander-in-chief will demand the same honor. Our text, 2 Thessalonians 2:3-4, makes this clear. "The son of perdition . . . opposeth and exalteth himself above all that is called God, or that is worshiped; so that he as God sitteth in the temple of God, showing himself that he is God."

Initially the Antichrist may show great toleration for various religions. We know he will give Israel the opportunity to rebuild the temple and resume its ancient animal sacrifices (Dan 9:27). But he will desecrate the temple and make himself the object of worship after three and one-half years, as we have just read.

Jesus predicted the abomination of the temple worship, just as Daniel did (Matt. 24:15). It will occur in the midst of the Tribulation, and everyone on earth will be required to worship the self-proclaimed messiah. Those who refuse will die, for they will be denied food. Only by accepting the mark of submission on their hands or foreheads will they be allowed to buy food and sell their labor. In this way the Antichrist will fulfill his monstrous design.

His Doom

The success of the Antichrist will be greater than any previous leader—for a time, and times, and the dividing of time. For three and one-half years he will control the nations despite a series of natural disasters sent from heaven. The "trumpet" judgments in Revelation 8—9 cause a third of the earth's trees to be burned and a third of the seas to turn rank with pollution.

Then the Jewish nation will rebel against their oppressor, and the infuriated Antichrist will lead his army against the rebels. Anti-Semitism, always inspired by Satan, the arch Jew-hater, will reach its fiercest pitch as the Antichrist races to annihilate the ancient people of God. But the idolaters' cup of iniquity is full and God will permit no more evil.

As Jerusalem's people are threatened, Jesus Christ will descend from heaven with invincible angelic armies, and the Jewish people will see the Man they pierced on the Cross and mourn their nation's rejection of the Messiah. Israel will be spared, and the long-promised King of righteousness will take up the scepter of the earth.

And the Antichrist? He is doomed. "The beast [Antichrist] was taken, and with him the false prophet that wrought miracles before him, with which he deceived them that had received the mark of the beast, and them that worshiped his image. These both were cast alive into a lake of fire burning with brimstone" (Rev. 19:20).

That's the last we hear of the Antichrist. He'll suffer forever for a few years of self-exaltation under the protection of Satan. Satan's power is second to God's supreme power. Antichrist and Satan and their followers are losers—forever.

8

The Good Society

Humanity through the ages has dreamed of a golden age of peace and prosperity. Philosophers and politicians have proposed ways to attain it, and poets and novelists have celebrated its beauties and delights. But this golden Utopia has never come, and today the prospects seem dimmer than ever.

In America we've seen Roosevelt's New Deal, Kennedy's New Frontier, and Johnson's Great Society come and go. The names change, but the pattern is the same: enthusiasm and disillusion; struggle and failure.

But the Golden Age is coming—God said it will. He also says He will establish it because humanity lacks the power and wisdom to create this sublime society.

The Certainty of the Good Society
Old Testament prophets give us vivid descriptions

of this ideal society: everyone will have enough food and clothing and housing; justice will be fair and prompt; animals will be pets and the birds will be singing; riots and wars will not destroy lives and cripple bodies. We'll look at these descriptions.

Jesus also spoke of this golden era and its government to His disciples. "In the regeneration when the Son of man shall sit on the throne of His glory, ye also shall sit upon twelve thrones, judging the twelve tribes of Israel" (Matt. 19:28). Just before His crucifixion, Jesus assured the Jewish high priest that His second coming to earth would display the power and glory of a king (Matt. 26:64).

The divine leadership of this future kingdom is confirmed in the prophecy of Daniel. You recall that Daniel was given a vision of a statue constructed of gold, silver, brass, and iron mixed with clay (Dan. 2). The metals represented four successive empires, an angel told Daniel, and they would be supplanted by a power that would fill the whole earth (v. 35).

The vanquishing force in the vision was "a stone cut out without hands," signifying its source is divine, not human. Then Daniel explains: "And in the days of these kings shall the God of heaven set up a kingdom, which shall never be destroyed: and the kingdom shall not be left to other people, but it shall break in pieces and consume all these kingdoms, and it shall stand forever" (v. 44).

We have seen that human achievements are not able to bring the kingdom of our Saviour on this earth. It will not even come about through the preaching of the Gospel. Today the greatest hope of our world is the preaching of the Gospel, for the Bible says it pleases the Lord to save people by the "foolishness of preaching." But as transforming as the Gospel is to change individual people who receive Christ and turn from sin, it does not change all people in this world. Gospel preaching is God's method of calling people to a heavenly citizenship, not to a reformed society.

Neither will the efforts of organized Christianity bring the kingdom of our Lord. When Christians cannot agree on Bible doctrines, it is futile to hope they can agree on a political program. In fact, the Bible reveals that the organized church of the last days will have a tendency toward apostasy. Churchmen will depart from the faith, embracing the doctrines of devils and heeding seducing spirits. Tragically, the organized church will betray the kingdom of our Lord.

Neither will the kingdom of Jesus Christ be built by social efforts in legislation, planning, and clean politics. These things are good and necessary for decent living, but they cannot wipe out the epidemic disease of sin. Selfishness, jealousy, and covetousness plague every program conceived by hopeful planners.

America's Peace Corps was a noble attempt to share modern skills and knowledge with deprived peoples of the earth. The objectives were economic prosperity and international peace, and doubtless the sacrificial efforts accomplished much good. But organizational strife and political intrigue corrupted the Peace Corps. Its members failed to maintain peace in their own ranks.

The Bible tells us that God is the God of peace (1 Thes. 5:23). Our experience should tell us that there is no enduring peace apart from God. God has a monopoly on peace. If you desire peace in your heart, you must get it from God. If the world wants peace between nations, it must make God its Sovereign.

The way to personal peace is given in Romans: "Being justified by faith, we have peace with God through our Lord Jesus Christ" (5:1). This peace fills a life when this admonition is heeded: "Be careful [anxious] for nothing; but in everything by prayer and supplication with thanksgiving let your requests be made known unto God. And the peace of God, which passeth all understanding, shall keep your hearts and minds through Christ Jesus" (Phil. 4:6-7). What God does for the individual He must do for the nations before there can be peace.

Not all Christians believe that the Bible promises a golden age, or a Millennium of peace and prosperity. These Christians hold the "amillennial" or the "postmillennial" views of Scripture. The "golden age" view I have described is held by the "premillennialists."

If someone had asked me which group I belonged to back in seminary days, I might have answered: "I am *pan*millennialist—I just think it's going to pan out all right." Maybe that's your view also, but the important thing is to know that you are a child of God, that heaven is your home, and that you are living for Him.

There is great value, however, in knowing about this teaching of the Word of God because it's such a significant part of the future.

The word "millennium" is a Latin word which means a thousand years. We encounter it six times in Revelation 20. The question is: What is the Millennium and how does it relate to Jesus' second coming?

Postmillennial view

Various theologians from Augustine to contemporary scholars interpret Christ's rule over the earth as a spiritual influence through His Church. They believe Christianity will improve world conditions over an indefinite period of time until Jesus returns to judge all people and establish His eternal kingdom.

This view dominated Christianity until the present century. Theologians were inclined to interpret prophecy in a symbolical way, and human progress in science and education encouraged optimism for the advancement of all civilization. Then came World War I, World War II, and the sceptre of World War III. Not even the social scientists are optimistic now about Earth's future.

Another problem with the postmillennial view is that it fails to account for the Bible statement that Satan will be bound during the Millennium. If we are in the Millennium now, Satan's power is shackled because Revelation 20:1-3 tells of a time when angels will bind Satan with a chain and seal him in the bottomless pit for one thousand years. Someone said if Satan is bound now, he's sporting the longest chain on record.

Amillennial View

Amillennialists, like premillennialists, believe the Scriptures teach about worsening instead of improving conditions on the earth before Jesus returns. Evil will become so strong, they believe, that only the powerful intervention of Christ can prevent chaos. But amillennialists interpret the "one thousand years" as being a figurative representation of the coming Kingdom and not as a literal 1,000 years. Amillennialists use such verses as Luke 1:31-33, ". . . and the Lord God shall give unto Him the throne of His father David: and He shall reign over the house of Jacob forever." They interpret "He shall reign . . . forever" as literal.

The most serious problem with amillennialism is the manner in which those who hold this view interpret Revelation 20. They spiritualize this passage, or take it to mean something less than literal. This is one passage among many others that the amillennialists—and the postmillennialists—spiritualize or interpret in a symbolic way.

I agree that many passages in Scripture are figurative in meaning—such as "the trees of the field shall clap their hands" for joy—but the throne of David and the house of Jacob are actual, historical entities. When interpreters reject the plain meaning of a passage, it is because their rigid theological system is threatened. We must apply evenly the rules of Scripture interpretation—figuratively where the intention is obviously figurative, and literally where obviously literal.

Premillennial view

The third view, which I accept, sees world conditions deteriorating as they did before the Flood, the return of Jesus to conquer the Antichrist and rescue the Jewish nation, and the establishment of a one-thousand-year kingdom with headquarters in Jerusalem. This view developed as Bible students began to interpret prophecy more literally and recognized the distinctive roles in history of Israel and the Church.

I believe a fair-minded consideration of the Scriptures is likely to lead Bible readers to the premillennial position. You have already read a good portion of its interpretations, and I trust you have found them consistent and reasonable. The Holy Spirit adds His special enlightenment, and I pray He will confirm the truth as I give you some marvels of the Millennium.

The Serenity of the Good Society

We've seen that Satan will be imprisoned during the Millennium. His absence from the world will make a tremendous difference in human conduct. No longer will the men and women who have survived the Tribulation be morally tempted by this evil being. His insidious and destructive influence is indicated by his names: dragon, serpent, devil ("accuser"), and Satan ("enemy"). People will still do wrong, but they won't be tricked or impelled by this ingenious traitor. As predicted, the "seed of the woman," Christ, has vanquished the "seed of the serpent," Antichrist, and the serpent himself.

Another momentous change will be the transformation of nature. When God created the world, everything was pronounced good. We can only imagine how lush and resplendent everything was when it came from the hand of God. But decay and death infected the whole creation when man sinned against his Maker. Genesis 3 tells of God's judgment: "Cursed is the ground for thy sake . . . thorns also and thistles shall it bring forth to thee" (vv. 17-18). Because of man's sin, incited by Satan, there are thorns on a rose and desert spots that support no life.

Paul, in figurative language, says the world is waiting for its day of liberation. "The earnest expectation of the creature [creation] waiteth for the manifestation of the sons of God. . . . For we know that the whole creation groaneth and travaileth in pain together until now" (Rom. 8:19, 22). Just as believers' bodies are to be freed from blemish and weakness, nature will be miraculously restored to harmony and purity.

For a glimpse of that new world of nature, we turn to Isaiah 35:1. "The wilderness and the solitary place shall be glad for them; and the desert shall rejoice, and blossom as the rose."

I once saw a science film that recorded the plant life of the desert with high-powered lens. The pictures revealed flowers in the sand as beautiful as any orchid you have ever seen. When the Lord Jesus Christ comes back to earth, our deserts will blossom as a rose under the perfect climatic conditions. And there's more.

"Then shall the lame man leap as an hart, and the tongue of the dumb sing; for in the wilderness shall waters break out, and streams in the desert. And the parched ground shall become a pool, and the thirsty land springs of water: in the habitation of dragons, where each lay, shall be grass with reeds and rushes" (Isaiah 35:6-7). What a paradise for anglers!

The animal kingdom is also going to be transformed. Today a balance in nature is maintained by animals that feed on others which in turn survive by fang and claw. Before the Flood, men did not fear animals, and the beasts ate plant food, not other animals.

In the millennial rule of Christ, astonishing changes will be seen. "The wolf also shall dwell with the lamb, and the leopard shall lie down with the kid; and the calf and the young lion and the fatling together; and a little child shall lead them. And the cow and the bear shall feed; their young ones shall lie down together: and the lion shall eat straw like the ox" (Isaiah 11:6-7).

Can you imagine a child leading a lion on a ribbon? And a baby petting a cobra? Those will be everyday scenes when the peacemaking Jesus removes all the fierceness of the animal kingdom.

Perfect justice will be another shining achievement of the millennial kingdom. This will flow from law courts supervised by honest and wise officials. The Chief Judge is Christ, and He will not permit corrupt administration or delayed retribution. The unknown will get as fair a hearing as the renowned.

We cannot examine all the wonders of the Millennium, but we cannot overlook what will be perhaps the greatest boon to human society. It is found in Isaiah 2:4. "And He [the Saviour] shall judge among the nations, and shall rebuke many people: and they shall beat their swords into plowshares, and their spears into pruninghooks: nation shall not lift up sword against nation, neither shall they learn war any more."

A great cry in our generation has sounded against war. As never before, ordinary men and women comprehend the horror and waste of warfare. The major powers have stockpiled nuclear weapons that can practically obliterate civilization. Medium-size nations possess atomic warheads that can trigger a holocaust anywhere on earth.

Jesus predicted there would be wars and rumors of wars while power-hungry leaders rule the earth, but weapons will not be needed or tolerated in a world ruled by justice and provided with plenty. At last, peace will prevail across the earth.

The greatest blessing of all during the Millennium is described in verse 9 of Isaiah 11. "They shall not hurt nor destroy in all my holy mountain: for the earth shall be full of the knowledge of the Lord, as the waters cover the sea."

Everyone will know the Lord in millennial days! No one will wonder what He's like or what pleases Him. They will see His love and power and wisdom, and they will worship and serve Him as they rest and work and prosper through long years of life. Some of the facts about the millennial kingdom are not clear from Scripture. For example, what will be the nature of those who return from heaven with Christ when He returns? Will there be children born during the Millennium? Will the millennial kingdom be perfect? If so, who will begin the war which will take place at the end of the millennial age? We don't know all the answers. But there will be a brief, final outbreak of rebellion against God, mobilized by Satan who is released from his dungeon for evil's last revolt. Satan will muster a surprising number of insurgents, but their attack will be crushed (Rev. 20:7-9).

How fearful is the power of sin! Knowledge about the Lord is no substitute for personal identification with Him by faith. If you have not surrendered your life to Him and been cleansed of your sins, all your knowledge about God can only condemn you. Until He is your Father by rebirth, you are the child of Satan by only one birth (John 8:42-44; 3:6-7).

9

The Great
White Throne

You've never seen a courtroom like it: the Judge, robed in dazzling light, looks down from a resplendent white throne; the defendant before Him hears a long list of charges and instantly admits his guilt; behind the hopeless felon stretches a line of mute prisoners that reaches out of sight. A scene like this looms at the end of the Good Society.

The most solemn and fearsome scene in all Scripture is the Great White Throne Judgment. The Bible's account of Sodom and Gomorrah's fiery destruction is awesome, and the devastating scourges of earth during the Tribulation are shocking, but the divine sentence of doom on eternal souls is almost too terrible for words. Yet it is a reality, and it is good for us to face up to the Great White Throne Judgment.

We discover several thrones of God in Scripture. His eternal throne: "The Lord hath prepared His throne in the heavens; and His kingdom ruleth over all" (Ps. 103:19). The award throne for Christians: "We shall all stand before the judgment seat of Christ" (Rom. 14:10). The decisions rendered here will reward Christians for their faithful service. Christ's throne of glory will assign judgments to nations that have persecuted the Jews during the tribulation. "When the Son of man shall come in His glory, and all the holy angels with Him, then shall He sit upon the throne of His glory" (Matt. 25:31). And Christ will rule from a throne in Jerusalem during the golden age. "And the Lord God shall give unto Him the throne of His father David" (Luke 1:32). Finally, there will be the dreaded Great White Throne.

God has clearly warned mankind that sinners will face a judgment day. The warning appears over and over in Scripture, and I believe it is also written in every human heart.

Some truths are self-evident; I call them first truths. We do not have to be taught these truths because God gives them to us intuitively. The fact that God exists is a first truth although atheistic propaganda frequently disclaims it.

The certainty of judgment is another first truth. The Bible tells us and experience confirms that humans instinctively sense the coming of judgment day. Many attempt to smother the knowledge, and modern society bombards us with denials, but the fear continues to lurk in most hearts. It is God's warning to us. The fateful day is described in the Revelation: "And I saw a great white throne, and Him that sat on it, from whose face the earth and the heaven fled away; and there was found no place for them" (Rev. 20:11). The identity of the one upon the throne must be the Lord Jesus Christ, for we are told that "the Father judgeth no man, but hath committed all judgment unto the Son" (John 5:22).

Jesus came to the world nearly 2,000 years ago as its Saviour; He came then in humility and love to extend God's mercy to mankind. He will come again in justice and judgment to sentence sinners who reject that love. The great question of our day is: What will you do with Jesus Christ? The question in that future day will be: What will Jesus Christ do with you?

The heaven and earth will flee away in the presence of the Judge, according to Revelation 20:11. I believe the earth will depart because it is stained with the blood of the Son of God. The heaven will shun His presence because it has been the abode of the kingdom of darkness. Suspended somewhere in space, the Great White Throne will be erected for Judgment Day.

The Prisoners

Who will be at the Great White Throne Judgment? I want to make very clear that no saved person will appear at the Great White Throne Judgment. All believers share in the first resurrection, as we saw in 1 Thessalonians 4. Their security is affirmed in Revelation. "Blessed and holy is he that hath part in the first resurrection: on such the second death hath no power" (Rev. 20:6). The child of God has "settled his case out of court"—he received forgiveness at the Cross.

The White Throne trial is appointed for unbelievers who couldn't share in the first resurrection. Their awakening is to "shame and everlasting contempt" (Dan. 12:2). John writes of them when he says: "I saw the dead, small and great, stand before God" (Rev. 20:12).

Adolf Hitler never came to trial on earth for his crimes, but he won't miss this court date. The unconvicted child murderer will be there. Infidels who scoffed at belief in God, corrupters of youth through drugs and sensuality, religious people who prided themselves on personal goodness, and procrastinators who delayed a decision for Christ one day too long—they'll all be there. Many kinds of sinners will be there—the despicable and the respectable—who disdained the blood of Jesus Christ for washing away their sins.

The Penalties

We might wonder how the trials will be conducted, and John informs us: "The books were opened, and another book was opened, which is the Book of Life. And the dead were judged out of those things which were written in the books, according to their works" (Rev. 20:12).

Many people yearn to preserve the experiences of their life in a biography. Writers traditionally include the accomplishments and characteristics that flatter the subject, and consequently readers do not see the real person. The books written in heaven are a different kind: they include every thought, and deed experienced in the individual's mind and body. The prospect is staggering—except for the cleansed, forgiven sinners who won't be there!

While watching a Moody Science film I was amazed to discover that the words we speak send sound signals into space, and that if we had sufficiently sensitive equipment we could recover from the atmosphere words which men spoke centuries ago! Spoken words are not lost in the ether, and at the Great White Throne Judgment they will come back to testify against their owner. Of course, the pleasant and helpful words will reecho also, as the book of deeds is a complete and accurate record.

I think another book that will be opened is the Word of God. Jesus indicated this when He described the future of the people who heard His words and rejected them. "The word that I have spoken, the same shall judge him in the last day" (John 12:48).

Today it is popular to judge God's Word. Intellectuals mock it, scientists contradict it, comedians profane it, and the self-serving masses ignore it. But the eternal Word won't go away, and one day God's changeless Word will be placed alongside men's lives to measure their perfection. The comparison will settle all disputes.

In Habakkuk we read: "The Lord is in His holy temple; let all the earth keep silence before Him" (2:20). We often use this verse to encourage reverence in church, but the primary meaning concerns the wickedness of humanity facing the holy God. All human defenses will crumble before the penetrating gaze of God. There is only one verdict: "Guilty as charged."

One final book is opened at the White Throne Judgment: the Lamb's Book of Life. The Lamb's Book of Life is the record of names of all who are redeemed through faith in the blood of the Lord Jesus Christ. After the personal accounts are read from the book of deeds, a check is made of the names in the Book of Life. "And there shall in no wise enter into it [New Jerusalem] any thing that defileth, neither whatsoever worketh abomination, or maketh a lie: but they which are written in the Lamb's Book of Life" (Rev. 21:27).

Is your name in the Book of Life? Some say, "My name is on the church membership roll; I sacrificed a lot for my church." Others say their name is in the social register, or "I made *Who's Who* one year." That doesn't count for salvation. Is your name in the Lamb's Book of Life? Do you possess Christ's life today through trusting Him as Lord and Saviour? If He's not your Saviour He will be your Judge.

"And whosoever was not found written in the Book of Life was cast into the lake of fire" (Rev. 20:15). The Great White Throne Judgment vindicates the holiness of God after centuries of revolt by His creatures. He will not allow wickedness forever, but His mercy will never end. You may receive it by inviting Christ into your heart.

10

Hell:
Straight Ahead

In our sophisticated day it is popular to joke about hell. Many people prefer to think of hell as a legend based on Dante's *Inferno* or Michelangelo's *Last Judgment* or Milton's *Paradise Lost* rather than an actual place described by Jesus. "Hell" remains in everyday vocabularies but is absent from most church sermons. Many consider it crude and unloving to even speak seriously about hell. But the Bible doesn't avoid it, and neither can I. After talking about God's judgment at the Great White Throne, it is natural for some people to ask: Is there really a place of torment where people go who reject Jesus Christ as their Saviour?

If hell is only a myth, Christianity needs a major reformation. If hell is not real, the Bible is not true. If there is no hell at the end of a wicked life, there is no heaven at the end of a God-fearing life. But if hell waits at the end of life's road, we'd better know about it.

Hell is not a pleasant subject to talk about. Nobody should speak about hell except with a broken heart of compassion for those who are lost in sin. But the unpleasantness of a subject does not change its actuality. I do not like to think about suffering, and yet suffering is a serious problem for us to face. I do not like to think about war casualties and yet war must be dealt with. Hell is just as real, and we can conquer it only by admitting it is there.

Its Reality

The King James Bible translates into English as "hell" four Hebrew and Greek words. In the Old Testament, the Hebrew word is Sheol. It usually means the grave or the abode of the dead. But some passages use Sheol as the abode of the *wicked* dead. For instance, "The wicked shall be turned into hell, and all the nations that forget God" (Ps. 9:17).

In the New Testament the Greek word for the place of the dead is Hades. It is used in Luke 16 in the story about the rich man who died and went to a place of torment.

The third term for a place of punishment is the Greek word *tartarus*. "God spared not the angels that sinned, but cast them down to hell, and delivered them into chains of darkness, to be reserved unto judgment" (2 Peter 2:4). Lucifer, the chief of the angels, led a rebellion against God that resulted in some angels being consigned to a special prison called *tartarus*.

The most prominent word used for hell in the New Testament is Gehenna. It was the name of a notorious valley on the southwest side of Jerusalem. In the days of Israel's idolatrous kings little children were offered there to the pagan god Moloch. The helpless victims were tossed into the red-hot arms of Moloch's iron statue, and their wailing gave the area the name, The Valley of Lamentations. King Josiah ended this barbarism and turned the narrow valley into a garbage dump. Dead animals and executed criminals were thrown into the valley along with the city's garbage. A steady fire burned and smoldered, consuming the combustible materials, and worms foraged on the remains. It was a loathsome place that Jesus chose to compare with the destination of wicked people.

"If thy hand offend thee, cut it off: it is better for thee to enter into life maimed, than having two hands to go into hell, into the fire that never shall be quenched: where their worm dieth not, and the fire is not quenched" (Mark 9:43-44). Those who reject God's offer of mercy, those who reject God's offer of salvation in the Lord Jesus Christ go to a terrible place called Gehenna. Thus, everytime we see a garbage dump, it ought to preach a sermon to us about hell.

When I was pastor in a rural church, I had to take our garbage to a county dump. I dreaded it everytime I went. The stench of the place was terrible. There was a fire licking continually, and mangy dogs picked through the filth. It always reminded me of Jesus' words. The garbage dumps of this life carry a warning about eternity, and we should heed that warning.

In addition to particular names for hell, repelling descriptions are given. It is called a place of everlasting fire, a furnace of fire, the bottomless pit, and the blackness of darkness forever. The people who joke about meeting all their friends in these surroundings had better enjoy their laughs now—there will be none in Hades.

Jesus Christ had the most compassionate heart that ever beat, and yet He had more to say about hell than any preacher after Him. The grimmest hell-fire, damnation preacher was not Jonathan Edwards or Billy Sunday; it was the Lord Jesus Christ. He did not take pleasure in the subject, but He warned men against going to hell because it is an awful reality.

Its Retribution

The justice of God demands that there be a hell. God is love, the Bible tells us, but He is also holy. "Behold therefore the goodness and severity of God" (Rom. 11:22). We will never fully fathom the love of God—it's limitless and it reaches toward men until it is finally rejected. Then God's holiness demands judgment.

Almost everyone has heard John 3:16—"For God so loved the world that He gave His only begotten Son, that whosoever believeth in Him should not perish, but have everlasting life." Here we see God's great love and His ultimate judgment in one verse. There are two choices before the world: everlasting life; and everlasting death, or "perishing." The second choice does not mean extinction of consciousness, but separation from everything desirable in life. Hell will be a living death.

The most frequent objection I hear to the existence of hell is: "You surely don't believe that a loving God would send anybody to a terrible place called hell!" And I reply, "I don't believe that God sends anybody to hell, but I believe sin sends men to hell."

When a person goes to hell, he goes in spite of the warning of his conscience; he goes in spite of the love of the Saviour who died for him; he goes in spite of the witness of Christians to him.

There was a boy in a southern state many years ago whose father lavished all he had on the lad. But something failed in the mind of the boy and he became criminally insane. Dangerous to his family and himself, he had to be incarcerated with the insane.

Hell is God's penitentiary for the spiritually incorrigible, His detention center for the spiritually insane. When a person refuses spiritual healing, he carries his sin-disease into the incurable ward of eternity.

So when we tell the truth about hell, it is an act of mercy. Wouldn't you be grateful if you were speeding down a road and a man waved you down at the risk of his own life just before your car plunged across a broken bridge? That's why I warn everyone I can about the peril of hell. And I speak in love.

Its Residents

How did hell come into being? The Bible says: "A fire is kindled in mine [God's] anger, and shall burn unto the lowest hell" (Deut. 32:22). God kindled the fire of hell for specific inhabitants. "Depart from Me, ye cursed, into everlasting fire, prepared for the devil and his angels" (Matt. 25:41).

The supreme God will eventually banish all evil and imperfection to the lake of fire. Satan and the Antichrist and the False Prophet will go first as the ones who deceived mankind (Rev. 20:10), and their followers will join them as willing allies (20:15).

Sinners of all kinds will get to heaven instead of hell, since "whosoever shall call upon the name of the Lord shall be saved" (Rom. 10:13). But every murderer who does not repent, every adulterer who does not bow to Jesus, every liar who is not cleansed, and every drunkard who lacks Calvary's cure will end in hell. Yes, and unforgiven thieves and extortioners as well as those who failed to love the Lord with all their hearts and their neighbor as themselves—and didn't care.

Jesus told a story that reveals much about the future consequences of sin. We know the details give an actual insight into death because Jesus mentioned a specific individual.

Lazarus was a poor man who ate leftovers from the table of an aristocrat. When the beggar died, however, ministering angels conveyed Lazarus into "Abraham's bosom," Jesus said. In other words, Lazarus received royal treatment as a member of the same family of faith as Abraham.

Before Jesus died and rose with a new body, the dead went to a place separated into two sections, as we see in this story. At Jesus' death, He descended to this divided waystation and took His people to the paradise above, according to Ephesians 4:8-10 and Luke 23:43. Lazarus was among them, but first he was due to glimpse the rich acquaintance under very different circumstances.

The rich man died and was buried, said Jesus, and undoubtedly he had a very impressive funeral service. Perhaps there was a long obituary on the public bulletin board. But he didn't receive special treatment in Hades.

"And in hell he lift up his eyes, being in torments and seeth Abraham afar off, and Lazarus in his bosom. And he cried and said, . . . Send Lazarus, that he may dip the tip of his finger in water, and cool my tongue, for I am tormented in this flame" (Luke 16:23-24).

In Greek mythology we find a story that portrays a refined form of torture. For his alleged sins, Tantalus was condemned to reach toward a sparkling lake to quench his thirst and always see the water ebb beyond his touch. And he was doomed to stretch for boughs of fruit and see them swept away from his grasp. Eternally tantalized; never fulfilled. It seems to imitate the real hell.

Rarely does an individual go to hell alone. He says, "I'll live as I want to live, and hurt no one but myself." But it didn't work that way for the rich man. He remembered his five brothers back on earth and said, "Father Abraham, send Lazarus that he may warn my five brothers that they come not to this place."

But no one could go back. And Abraham assured him it would be useless for one to return from the dead if the living would not listen to the prophets in the Scriptures!

Today there's no news from hell, but there's good news from the Scriptures. You and I do not have to go to hell: Jesus Christ took our hell for us. At the cross of Calvary Jesus took the sins of the world on His own soul (1 Peter 3:18). For three hours darkness covered the earth, and Jesus Christ went through hell's furies, wrenching from Him the cry: "My God, My God, why hast Thou forsaken me?" Jesus was forsaken so we won't need to be forsaken.

I don't have trouble believing in the existence of hell. What surpasses my logic is the glorious news that we hell-deserving sinners don't have to go there, but we can go to God's heaven. Thank God we are not saved by logic, but by love.

No one has to go to hell—if he turns off the road through the narrow gate of faith. Jesus waits there, beckoning. Anyone may enter His heaven. Will you?

11

Heaven at Last

Home and family mean different things to different people, but there is always something wonderful to me about going home. I recall how my emotions surged when I returned home after four years in college. I was turning my back on one period in my life and entering another that was to start from a place I love. What comfort and encouragement I expected at home! I could hardly wait to arrive!

I think that's the way it is with the people of God who have gotten some bruises in the world and they begin to realize God has a home waiting for them that is filled with understanding and love and joy. That's heaven, our home for eternity, and perhaps we'd be more eager to take that trip if we knew more about heaven.

Just as the Bible warns us of a hell to shun, it assures us of a wonderful heaven to gain. God gave John a vision on the Island of Patmos of what heaven will be like. We can glimpse enough of its glory to heighten our praise for God's majestic provision.

We are told in the Book of Hebrews that Abraham, one of the great heroes of the faith, looked forward to the day when he would move to his permanent home above. A tent-dweller moving from place to place with his flocks, he considered himself a pilgrim looking for a city whose builder and maker was God. Abraham knew his God would construct a magnificent home for His people, though he had no details such as we have in the later revelations.

A Prepared Place

Jesus said, "Let not your heart be troubled: ye believe in God, believe also in Me. In My Father's house are many mansions. . . . I go to prepare a place for you. And if I go and prepare a place for you, I will come again, and receive you unto Myself" (John 14:1-3). Perhaps 60 years after giving this promise, Jesus permitted the vision which the apostle records in Revelation.

"And I John saw the holy city, new Jerusalem, coming down from God out of heaven, prepared as a bride adorned for her husband" (Rev. 21:2). Heaven is a prepared place, and so I want to take a quick tour of this new city, with John as our guide.

Did you notice the name of our future home? New Jerusalem. That's very significant. Jerusalem in Israel was the earthly home of God, the place He chose for making known His power and glory. It was also the city of peace, celebrated far and wide for its dedication to justice among men. Jerusalem was famed for its beautiful buildings that glowed with a golden hue in the sunlight. And it is revered in the hearts of Christians for marking God's supreme expression of love for mankind: Jesus' death on the cross. New Jerusalem will continue to be the holy city in a special way.

New Jerusalem will also have a wall around it, but its 250-foot, jeweled height will focus attention on its glory, not protect the residents from enemies.

The wall has three gates on each side, gates made of pearl. The people of God will enter the city through the northern gates, the southern gates, the eastern and the western. And entering through the pearly gates will remind us, I think, of the cost involved in bringing us to heaven.

Salvation is free but it is not a cheap salvation. It took the lifeblood of Jesus on the cross to pay for my redemption. A pearl speaks of this high cost because it is formed through suffering.

The beautiful pearls we wear began as irritating sand grains in the shells of oysters. The grains cut into the oyster, stimulating a secretion which gradually enveloped the foreign element and created prized jewels.

Our Saviour willingly took upon Himself the sins of the world and covered them with his blood. We who accept the covering are jewels that shine for God, and I'll remember my Saviour when I walk past those pearl gates.

We see that the street of heaven is made of transparent gold (21:21). What a contrast with our earthly scene! Down here men worship gold and they trod over God, but in heaven we'll worship God and literally walk on gold.

We'd expect the city to have a lighting system —but none like this. The sun is dim beside the radiance issuing from Jesus, the shining Light of New Jerusalem (v. 23). There'll be no night and no slackening of activity for recuperation—just one eternal day doing what we enjoy most.

And look at that river of pure water flowing from the throne of God and of Christ—it's as clear as crystal (22:1). It is called the water of life. Nearby is a fruit tree, and we're told it bears twelve different kinds of fruit. Such a tree is hard to imagine, but I'm sure the variety will be perfect for all tastes.

You can see that New Jerusalem is a carefully prepared community. And I feel that I'm getting prepared too.

A Populous Place

One of the thrilling things about heaven will be its multitudes of people. John glimpsed the future population and said they were beyond counting (Rev. 7:9). They come from every nation and language, and they mingle with myriads of angels. No gathering on earth ever saw individuals moving independently with such harmony.

This reminds me of the question I am frequently asked: "Are we going to know one another when we get to heaven?" Sometimes I hear it from parents who have lost a little baby. Or it is asked by the bereaved of a beloved mate.

The answer is a blessed "Yes," on solid biblical teaching. The Scripture declares that we shall know in heaven even as we are known (1 Cor. 13:12). While this primarily applies to knowledge of God, it indicates the individuality of personal relationships. We also know that specific names are listed in the Lamb's Book of Life.

When Jesus was on the mountain of transfigura-
tion with Peter, James, and John, the identity of
Moses and Elijah was recognized by the disciples
when these ancient prophets appeared. All the evidence indicates that we will recognize one another
in heaven.

What a thrilling reunion of the family of God!
We'll meet people we know by name and deed, and
lovely individuals with no claim to fame. You prob-
ably have picked the Bible personality you want to
chat with first. And there are sterling individuals
from church history we will want to befriend—
they died in flames or painted a great picture or
led the person to Christ who led us to Him!

Recognizing others will be a great joy in heaven,
and recognizing Jesus will be the sublimest encounter of all. The most gracious, most loving, most
winsome being in New Jerusalem will be our
Saviour. I think it will be hard to turn our eyes
away from our incomparable Lord. In all the multi-
tude of old friends and new acquaintants, Jesus
will stand out. I am longing to see His face.

A Perfect Place

The Apostle John graphically describes the perfection of heaven by the absence of some things, that
now mark our lives. "God shall wipe away all tears
from their eyes" (21:4). The tears of disappoint-
ment, tears of pain, tears of shame, and tears of
bereavement sprinkle our days and nights, and no
human is long immune.

A great preacher and medical doctor of past
days, Lynn Broughton, told how he visited a young
man in the hospital and tried to comfort him. The
patient was incurably ill with cancer, and the pas-

tor began talking about the Saviour and the heaven that was just ahead. Tears began to trickle from the young man's eyes, and the pastor wiped them with his handkerchief. "Just think," exclaimed the still-weeping man, "the next time these tears are wiped away, my heavenly Father will do it!"

The Scripture continues: "Neither will there be any pain." Just imagine how different that will be! We all know pain, both our own and of those around us. No hospitals, doctors, or drug stores will be necessary up there. No bodies will be handicapped or frail.

I knew of a child who was crippled from birth, and as she grew up watched other children play vigorously and she questioned why this had happened to her. "Auntie, why did God make me like this?" she queried. The godly woman answered, "Listen, Dear; I want you to know that God is not through making you yet. He's still working on you."

God's handicraft is not finished in this life. He's a master worker, and all those physical ailments will disappear at His touch when they have served His high purpose.

And, of course, death will be absent from heaven. Funerals are a very sad part of my ministry. When I was a boy, I said I'd never go to a wedding or a funeral. My wife and God changed that!

Death has to be faced, but it is a terrible enemy. Sin is the seed of death, and when we are delivered from the presence of sin we'll wave good-bye to death. That's the victory Jesus has gained for us in His prepared home.

When I was a boy we moved from one place to another until we were able to purchase a house and settle down. There we got comfortable and began enjoying the surroundings that belonged to us. A permanent home is assured us in heaven—no one will oust us, and no housing will look better.

So we're there, in perfect surroundings—just sitting, or playing harps? The Bible says, "They may rest from their labours" (Rev. 14:13), but it also says, "And His servants shall serve Him" (Rev. 22:3). Life in New Jerusalem will be more active and fulfilling than anything experienced on this earth. We creatures were made for full expression of our abilities, and they will unfold incredibly in the perfect environment of heaven. I can hardly wait to discover all that God meant me to be!

12

"Come Quickly, Lord Jesus"

Heaven is ready for God's people. It has been prepared by Jesus for us. My understanding of Scripture and of current events tells me that Jesus could return at any time for His Church. Then the world would plunge into the calamitous events we now see looming on the horizon.

One of the clear signs of the end times for me is the Club of Rome. It was founded by an Italian industrialist, Aurelio Peccei, who believes the critical problems of civilization must be met on a worldwide scale. The businessmen, scientists, and social planners who make up the informal membership of the Club of Rome have issued a 1976 report on international policies which *Time* magazine calls "an intellectual bombshell" (April 26, 1976 *Time*).

Instead of discouraging economic and population growth, as in its three-million copy book, *Limits to Growth*, the revised position urges selective growth of the economies in advanced and under-

121

developed nations in order to achieve a better balance of the earth's resources and productive
capacities. "The desired result," *Time* states, "could
lead to global peace and prosperity through economic interdependence."

To aid the planning, a computer model is being
fed data on population, food, energy, and climate
factors in ten regions of the world. Scientists will
develop test projects to see if computers can pre-
scribe reallocations of production that bring mutual
benefit to cooperating countries.

The ominous alternative to world cooperation,
warn the club members, is that mankind will rush
lemminglike to the disasters of war, starvation,
and suffocation predicted earlier by the Club of
Rome.

Martin Luther once said, "The devil is God's
ape." Whenever God offers a gift to mankind, Satan
dangles a gaudy counterfeit just beyond men's
grasp—and right above a spiritual precipice. World
government is one of these chasms—not that world
peace is bad, but that Satan's world leader will be
a fraud.

Events at the end time are something like a jig-
saw puzzle with many similar pieces. Let's see if
the larger pieces are fitting together in the pattern
that resembles the Bible picture. Remember that
these are not signs pointing to the Rapture of the
Church, but to later events ushering in the revelation of Christ to earth.

Anarchy

One of the puzzle pieces is anarchy. Jesus predicted, "And because iniquity shall abound, the
love of many shall wax cold" (Matt. 24:12). Some

translations put it: "And because lawlessness shall abound . . ." This points to a disintegration of authority and of respect for law. When anarchy moves in, authority moves out.

A modern joke tells about a man who went into a store to buy a Christmas toy for his child and the sales clerk said, "I want to show you a new educational toy. The purpose of the toy is to help children adjust to the times in which we live, so no matter how you put the parts together it comes out wrong." That would be funny if it weren't so realistic. So many things seem to be out of shape. Some elements of our society have been described as an insane asylum with the inmates trying to run it.

Consider the world of art. I do not know very much about art, but I become very concerned when a chimpanzee can overturn paint buckets on a canvas and smear it around with paws and nose with enough style to win an award for excellence from art critics. This reportedly happened, and it is not strange when symmetry and design and order break down as has happened in the structure of art.

And you're aware of the reading assignments in schools today that come under the category of "literature." I was reminded of this moral pollution when I saw a sign on a country road: "Dirt for sale." Dirt has its place, which is not in the minds of humans unless you want a crop of lust and rape and bestiality.

This filth floods the magazine racks and the best-selling books produced by our "most brilliant" authors. Much of it is straight pornography, and our moral standards are so decimated that the

Supreme Court of the United States declares it can no longer define "obscenity." The justices came to that conclusion only after removing most legal restrictions that helped protect young minds from this sewage.

I taught school a few years ago and the atmosphere was changing then. Veteran teachers have witnessed a revolutionary shift in education. Discipline is a major problem in many school systems of our nation. The prevailing philosophy is to coax or intrigue students into learning, and if that fails, to give up on educating the little darlings. Modern psychology doesn't know enough about human nature to realize that pampered darlings become obnoxious adults—if not criminals.

Apostasy

Apostasy is a half-dollar word meaning "religious treason." We don't see this yet, but the seeds seem to be planted. You recall that Paul said the day of the Lord would not arrive "except there come a falling away first" (2 Thes. 2:3). Organized Christianity is tilting, if not falling, away from its Lord.

Today the big church agencies stress sociology and politics, not the Cross of Calvary. Salvation is programmed through legislation and guerrilla warfare to give the underdog a bigger share of the world's pie. Sensing a threat to their bread and caviar, prominent financial supporters of denominational programs are squeezing the supply line. These Protestant denominations which neglect or disdain the biblical Gospel are beginning to gasp for spiritual breath. The tragedy is that many of their leaders don't know rigor mortis has set in.

The greatest church organization of all, Roman

Catholicism, is quivering on its foundation. Priests and nuns are deserting their vows, communicants are confused about which dogmas to discard and which to retain, and some Catholic theologians are challenging the supremacy of their pope. This 1,600-year-old institution shows astounding cracks in its structure.

Many church officials still dream of the day when Christendom will be united in one organization. That won't be possible until more rank and file members are willing to surrender the distinctive doctrines of their faith, but some church leaders are ready now for this giant step into a world church. To them, power is more godly than doctrinal teachings.

But the true Church, genuine believers in Jesus Christ, is seeing spiritual renewal. Home groups and church congregations all over this country are giving themselves to diligent Bible study, earnest intercessory prayer, and widening efforts to win people to Jesus Christ. They sense the birth pangs of a new era, and they are beginning to look more eagerly for the return of the Lord Jesus Christ. They belong to various denominations, and their "trademark" is their love for Jesus Christ. While the nominal church looks around for a super-leader, these people of God are anticipating reunion with their Lord!

Antichrist—Armageddon

How can one man take over the world? That is hard to imagine with our present international rivalries, babel of languages, and vacillating leaders. But the emergence of a world personality will be inevitable when commerce and communications shrink the globe while magnifying its problems. All nations will recognize the need for a political savior, and Satan will push his candidate onstage. Backed by diabolic publicity and Satan's own power, Antichrist cannot lose—until he faces Christ Himself at Armageddon.

Prophecy does not make clear whether atomic weapons will be used at the world's last war, but present arms buildup make nuclear conflagration a fearful possibility in the near future.

Israel possessed 13 atomic bombs and almost used them against her Arab attackers in the early stages of 1973's Yom Kippur War, according to *Time* magazine. More than a dozen nations have the materials and scientific capability of producing nuclear warheads, and some of them are not noted for political stability.

Iran, the Muslin but non-Arabic oil reservoir in the Mideast, is leaping toward military supremacy in its region. Exchanging oil dollars for weapons, the Shah of Iran plans to spend 10 billion dollars on weapons by 1980. His ruling passion is the restoration of Iran to its ancient glory under Cyrus the Great and Darius. Some day he may challenge the power of Russia and the United States.

According to *Israel My Glory* (February-March 1975), the *Jerusalem Post* printed a fascinating appraisal of Messiah-fever by a staff member Moshe Kohn. The *Post* reporter researched the writings of Talmudic sages who studied the times of Jesus, Bar-Kochba, and other revolutionary figures in Jewish history. Some of the sages' predictions for future messianic conditions were:

"Rabbi Yohanan: 'Wise people will be few and far between; the rest of us—our eyes will be weary

from grief and travail; troubles and terrible events will follow each other in quick succession.'

"Rabbi Yehuda: 'Impudence will abound, inflation will be rampant . . . the schools will be brothels; people will hold their nose in the presence of scholarship; piety will be despised; the young will humiliate the old; family members will hate each other; the leadership will be a doglike leadership.'"

These scholars were not necessarily looking for Jesus, but their descriptions cast the shadow of "the time of Jacob's trouble," as foretold in Jeremiah 30:7. Jesus called it "great tribulation, such as was not since the beginning of the world" (Matt. 24:21). Antichrist will spearhead Satan's hatred against God's chosen nation, and at Armageddon the world leader of the wicked will meet his doom (Rev. 19:11, 19-20).

Appearing
"As the lightning cometh out of the east, and shineth even unto the west, so also shall the coming of the Son of man be. . . . Immediately after the tribulation of those days shall the sun be darkened, and the moon shall not give her light, and the stars shall fall from heaven, and the powers of the heavens shall be shaken: and then shall appear the sign of the Son of man in heaven, and then shall all the tribes of the earth mourn, and they shall see the Son of man coming in the clouds of heaven with power and great glory" (Matt. 24:27, 29-30).

"And His feet shall stand in that day upon the mount of Olives, which is before Jerusalem in the east, and the mount of Olives shall cleave in the midst thereof toward the east and toward the

west . . . and the Lord my God shall come, and all the saints. . . . And the Lord shall be king over all the earth: in that day shall there be one Lord, and His name one" (Zech. 14:4-5, 9).

Glory! Are you ready for all this? There's only one way to get ready: make Jesus your Saviour now if you have never answered His knock at your heart's door (Rev. 3:20); and if you're a Christian, make Jesus Lord over every part of your life so you can win other men and women and boys and girls to Him through your witness.

The early Christians did not build the Church through half-hearted efforts, and neither will we. The harvest is ripe, the summer is ending, and many are not saved. May God make you a rejoicing part of His great ingathering. Even so, come quickly, Lord Jesus!